ON THE RUN IN SIBERIA

D1008017

ON THE RUN

IN SIBERIA

Rane Willerslev

Translated by Coilín ÓhAiseadha

University of Minnesota Press
Minneapolis • London

STATENS
KUNSTRÅD
DANISH ARTS COUNCIL

The translation of this book has been sponsored by
the Danish Arts Council Committee for Literature.

Originally published in Danish as *På flugt i Sibirien: Zobeljagt,
russisk mafia og 65 minusgrader* (Copenhagen: Gyldendal, 2009).

Published by the University of Minnesota Press
111 Third Avenue South, Suite 290
Minneapolis, MN 55401-2520
http://www.upress.umn.edu

Library of Congress Cataloging-in-Publication Data
Willerslev, Rane
[På flugt i Sibirien. English]
On the run in Siberia / Rane Willerslev ; translated by Coilín ÓhAiseadha.
Includes bibliographical references.
ISBN 978-0-8166-7626-2 (hardcover : alk. paper)
ISBN 978-0-8166-7627-9 (pbk. : alk. paper)
1. Yukaghir—Hunting—Russia (Federation)—Siberia. 2. Yukaghir—
Russia (Federation)—Siberia—Social life and customs. 3. Willerslev, Rane,
1971—Travel—Russia (Federation)—Siberia. 4. Refugees—Russia (Federation)—
Siberia—Biography. 5. Anthropologists—Denmark—Biography. 6. Sable
trapping—Russia (Federation)—Siberia. 7. Fur trade—Russia (Federation)—
Siberia. 8. Mafia—Russia (Federation)—Siberia. 9. Siberia (Russia)—Description
and travel. 10. Siberia (Russia)—Social life and customs. I. Title.
DK759.Y8W54 2012
305.89'46—dc23 [B]   2012001201

Design and composition by Yvonne Tsang at Wilsted & Taylor Publishing Services

Printed in the United States of America on acid-free paper

The University of Minnesota is an equal-opportunity educator and employer.

20 19 18 17 16 15 14 13 12   10 9 8 7 6 5 4 3 2 1

To the memory of Babushka Akulina

CONTENTS

PREFACE AND ACKNOWLEDGMENTS

The story you are about to read had its beginnings in 1993, when my identical twin brother, Eske, and I went on an expedition to northeastern Siberia with a small group of researchers and a film crew to study the Yukaghirs, an indigenous group of hunters who live in the northern part of the Russian Republic of Sakha (Yakutia). We were only twenty-two years old. I had started studying anthropology, and Eske, biology, at university a year earlier. We were already seasoned adventurers of the region, having spent the previous two years exploring various river systems of northeastern Siberia by canoe and learning how to survive by hunting. Because of this previous experience in Siberia, Eske and I helped organize and lead the expedition in 1993. After being dropped in the wilderness by helicopter, the expedition paddled for three and a half months along the Korkodon and Bolshoy Kuropatka Rivers. The aim was to find the Yukaghirs and to conduct ethnographic, linguistic, and biological research among them. We also were to collect Yukaghir cultural artifacts for an exhibition at the Moesgaard Prehistoric Museum in Denmark. All of this was filmed by the crew from Nordisk Film.[1]

I had first learned of the Yukaghirs when reading Waldemar Jochelson's classic monograph, *The Yukaghir and the Yukaghirized Tungus*,[2] which I found in a remote corner of the library of the Danish National Museum. The Yukaghirs described by Jochelson at the turn of the twentieth century fascinated me: they were the earliest indigenous people known to live in northeastern Siberia, and their language had no evident link to any known language group. Unlike other Siberian peoples, they had never domesticated animals as a food source; instead they survived their brutal environment exclusively through hunting. Meeting them fulfilled my youthful fantasy of seeking out a primordial and almost unknown hunter-gatherer people.

During our four-month expedition, we made contact with Yukaghir hunters in the forest and with a larger group living in the village of Nelemnoye. I came to know and love the Yukaghirs as friends and real individuals, generous people who welcomed us into their lives and protected me from danger. I also saw that their situation in post-Soviet Russia was desperate: these people were on their knees. The Yukaghirs lived in poverty as sable hunters, under the subjugation of the state fur-trading corporation, Sakhabult, which essentially operated as a regional Mafia syndicate. Their village leader, Nikolay ("Kolya") Shalugin, explained to us how Sakhabult had monopolized the area's fur trade since the fall of Communism, underpaying the hunters and preventing crucial deliveries of food, weapons, and ammunition to the Yukaghirs. Without essentials, hunters were forced to stay in the village, where they were drinking their lives away on cheap booze that was delivered to them by Russian traders. The youth were in despair, with hardly any access to education and a terribly high suicide rate, especially among the young men. The women, for the most part, preferred to establish romantic partnerships with Russians in the regional center Zyryanka, leaving the young hunters as bachelors with no hope of ever marrying. Tuberculosis, practically eradicated a few years previously, had now resurged as an epidemic, killing off young and old in every family.

I could not sit and listen passively to Shalugin's talk of horror. After returning to Copenhagen, I was determined to do something to help Shalugin and his hunters and to give them a better life.

I am not someone who would be called a political activist. I am quite uninterested in politics, and in my own political position I find the left almost as unappealing as the right; with seductive rhetoric and the assurance of improving life for the masses, both groups have all too often been insincere, guided by their own ambitions and short-sighted goals. My efforts to help the Yukaghirs were inspired by broader ideals of democracy and cooperative thinking, as well as my passion for studying the lives of hunting peoples in remote and isolated parts of the world and my inherent desire for adventure. I believed the Yukaghir hunters should be organized into a cooperative society, a business model well known and successful in Denmark. Together, as a collective, I imagined that they could effectively resist Sakhabult's exploitation by selling their sable pelts directly on the world market. Together with my friend Uffe Refslund Christensen, who had experience in the international fur trade, I established the Danish–Yukaghir Fur Project and worked with the changing leaders of the Yukaghirs. By this time I was also pursuing a doctorate in anthropology at Cambridge University (focused on Yukaghir religious beliefs) and learning Russian so that I could communicate directly with the hunters. The fur project seemed well planned and reasonable—at least in Denmark. It was the first of its kind in Siberia, where the fur trade had always been controlled by people other than the hunters: first by the czar, then by the Communist central government, and today by the Mafia, which skims the cream off the hunters' all too harsh and exhausting work in the wilderness. But it is not straightforward or simple to end more than three hundred years of brutal exploitation of Siberian hunters. Our grand project went awfully wrong.

The hardships I endured as a result of my failed fur project changed the core of my being. My father was a scientist, a man of reason. From him I had learned respect for objective knowledge, an aversion for misrepresentation, a dread of self-deception, and a yearning for clarity. But out among the hunters in the Siberian wilderness, I gradually lost my faith in reason. In this harsh environment, where supply lines have broken down and people have been forced back to a pure subsistence economy, life is sustained by something as irrational and fundamental as trust between humans and spirits. I learned to appreciate this way of thinking: if I had let myself be ruled by reason alone, I would surely be lying dead somewhere in the Siberian frost. A guardian angel, or what is known in Siberia as a *pomoshchnik,* a helping spirit, must have held a protective hand over me on more than one occasion. Although some people would call this romantic nonsense, this is precisely the heart of the matter, for my fur project was from the outset a romantic—perhaps even reckless —enterprise.

On a personal level, I believe every human being must celebrate existence, the fact that he or she is alive and has been given a life to fully appreciate. In my case, life brought me critically hazardous experiences in the Siberian wilderness, and I will not lie on my deathbed regretting that adventure eluded me. Yet only now, almost ten years after the fur project reached its dramatic climax, can I write the story down. These events, while exciting and adventurous, left scars on my soul. I have never been so close to death as during my time as a refugee in the taiga, and I have never been so starved and desperate as when trying to escape from the frost-hardened wilderness. At the time it was happening, I had no idea how it would all end. Only now do my memories constitute a completed whole, and I can begin to make out the chain of cause and effect that runs through my story. In the end, it is a matter of distance in time: anxiety and desperation fade as the years pass, and a sense of peace gradually spreads over what has happened. I now am able to remember and to write it down.

Yet I cannot avoid feeling a deep insecurity: how much do the Siberia I experienced at close hand and the Siberia I describe on the pages of this book actually have in common? It is difficult to remember all the details and nuances in the flowing, chaotic sensory impressions that concrete experiences become. I refer to my diary entries, but often I was so exhausted that I could not manage to write any more than the most essential, cursory, and factual information. I frequently have been forced to recall my thoughts and my state of mind anew after several years and the intervening experiences of my life.

Perhaps this is not a problem; when it comes down to it, life is determined by how it is remembered. I hope that the reader will trust my memory and follow along on my journey as an anthropologist, fur trapper, and refugee in Siberia.

■   ■   ■

Many people contributed to the creation of this book. My greatest thanks go to the Yukaghirs and to my friends in Siberia. Here,

I remember in particular Akulina and Gregory Shalugin, Alexandra and Ivan Danilov, Spiridon, Yura, and Peter Spiridonov, Slava Shadrin, Slava Sinitskiy, Kolya and Dusha Shalugin, Vasiliy Shalugin, and Nikolay Likhachev (Igor Khan). Next I express deep thanks to my friend and partner Uffe Refslund Christensen, and to journalist Lasse Lauridsen, who interviewed several members of the 1993 expedition and gave me invaluable help in the shaping of several chapters.

I thank Jesper Lauersen from Moesgaard Museum, and Bodil Selmer, Christian Suhr Nielsen, Bjarke Nielsen, and Ton Otto from the Department of Anthropology at Aarhus University for reading and commenting on the manuscript. I owe special thanks in this regard to Marie Højlund Bræmer and Dorte Heurlin. I also thank my longtime friend Coilín ÓhAiseadha, who translated this book from Danish to English with great stamina and professionalism. Thanks also to Santa Vizule for her help with the spelling of Russian words. I gratefully acknowledge the work of Marie Carsten Pedersen and of Jens Kirkeby and Sara Heil Jensen from the Moesgaard Museum, who produced the maps and drawings of ethnographic items and contributed the drawings that complement the text of the book. Jens Kirkeby illustrated Appendixes A, C, D, and E, and Sara Heil Jensen created the drawing for Appendix B. Thanks to the staff of the ethnographic collections at Moesgaard Museum, who kindly went to the storerooms to find the ethnographic items needed for drawing. I also thank these institutions and funds for generous support for my research among the Yukaghirs: the Danish Free Research Council, Crown Prince Frederik's Fund, Queen Margrethe and Prince Henrik's Fund, and the committee Nature and Peoples in the North.

Finally, I would like to thank my wife, Astrid Kjeldgaard-Pedersen, who encouraged me to write this book, and my daughters, Gertrud Akulina and Thyra Johanne Willerslev; all have tolerated my absence and have been an endless source of delight and inspiration along the way.

Abasy	the Devil (Sakha)
a'lma	shaman (Yukaghir)
ayibii	shadow; soul (Yukaghir)
Ayibii-lebie	the realm of the dead, or Land of Shadows (Yukaghir)
babushka	grandmother (Russian)
Barguzin	type of sable fur (English, from Russian Barguzinskiy)
Bulchut	fur-trading corporation founded by Anatoliy Maksimov (literally "hunter," Sakha)
Buyun	fur-trading corporation founded by the Russian Association of Indigenous Peoples of the North, RAIPON, in 2004 (Sakha)
chuchelo	puppet or mannequin (Russian)
dusha	soul (Russian)
Ilken	newspaper based in Yakutsk (Evenki)
koumiss	fermented mare's milk (English, from Sakha)
Lebie'-po'gil	the spirit owner of the forest (Yukaghir)
metvetiatnik	a hunter who has made himself a target for revenge by killing bears (literally "bear-marked," Russian)
Nelemnoye	a Yukaghir village on the Upper Kolyma River (Russian, from Yukaghir)

obshchina	commune, collective (Russian)
pe'jul	luck; hunted animal's guardian spirit or owner (Yukaghir)
promyshlenniki	contract workers in the fur trade in Siberia in the 1790s (English, from Russian)
Sakhabult	the Yakutian state fur-trading corporation (literally "Sakha prey," Sakha)
shatun	rogue bear that emerges from its den in winter to seek prey (Russian)
Soyuzpushnina	international fur auction in St. Petersburg, formerly known as Leningrad (Russian)
Teki Odulok	pseudonym of the Yukaghir writer Nikolay Spiridonov; also used as the name of the Yukaghirs' trading collective, or obshchina (Yukaghir)
tovarishch	comrade (Russian)
toyon	military clan leader (Sakha)
Uazik	a Russian make of jeep (Russian)
valenki	felt boots (Russian)
Verkhne Kolymsk	a village situated at the confluence of the Yasachnaya and Kolyma rivers (Russian)
Vezdekhod	a Russian make of personal tank (Russian)
Yakutsk	capital of the Sakha (Yakutia) Republic (Russian)
yasak	fur tax (Russian)
Zyryanka	a town on the Kolyma River, in an area once infamous for its Stalinist-era labor camps (Russian)

GALLERY OF CHARACTERS

ESKE WILLERSLEV: The author's twin brother, with whom he has traveled on several expeditions to Siberia. Eske is professor of evolutionary biology at Copenhagen University.

UFFE REFSLUND CHRISTENSEN: The author's friend and partner in the Danish–Yukaghir Fur Project. He works at the Kopenhagen Fur auction house and knows the international fur market.

KOLYA SHALUGIN (Yukaghir): First director of the Teki Odulok *obshchina* (commune), until he had to resign because of accusations of corruption. He visited Copenhagen with his wife, Dusha, and daughter, Alesha. The name "Kolya" is a diminutive of "Nikolay."

DUSHA SHALUGIN (Sakha): Wife of Kolya Shalugin.

MAKSIM SHALUGIN (Yukaghir): Kolya and Dusha Shalugin's oldest son.

IVAN DANILOV (Sakha): Unemployed electrician. He was born in the village of Aralakh and moved to Nelemnoye in the 1970s. He and the author lived alone together in the wilderness for several months after the author fled from the police.

SLAVA SINITSKIY (Russian): Proprietor of the only store in Nelemnoye. He is a friend of the Spiridonov family and Ivan Danilov. He helped the author to flee from the police and out into the wilderness.

SLAVA SHADRIN (Yukaghir): Assumed management of the Teki Odulok *obshchina* after Kolya Shalugin. Educated at the university in Yakutsk, he also works as a schoolteacher in Nelemnoye.

AKULINA SHALUGIN: The author's Yukaghir "grandmother," who made his fur clothes and looked after him with affection.

GREGORY SHALUGIN (Yukaghir): Husband of Akulina Shalugin. An elderly hunter who is deaf, he made the author's fur-covered skis and lent him his rifle.

NIKOLAY DANILOV (Sakha): Former mayor of Zyryanka and a childhood friend of Kolya Shalugin.

ALI IRISHKHANOV (nicknamed "Dudayev"): Chechen police chief in Zyryanka with connections to Sakhabult.

GERMAGEN (Sakha): He lives in Aralakh and is related to Ivan Danilov. He trained as a veterinarian in Moscow and has a special interest in the Danish philosopher Søren Kierkegaard.

SPIRIDON SPIRIDONOV (Yukaghir): The greatest moose hunter among the Yukaghirs, he died at the age of about eighty in 2000.

YURA SPIRIDONOV (Yukaghir): Spiridon's oldest son. He is a hunter and vice president of the Teki Odulok *obshchina*.

PETER SPIRIDONOV (Yukaghir): A hunter and Spiridon's youngest son.

ROSA (Sakha): Dusha Shalugin's youngest sister, with whom the author had a love affair.

IGOR KHAN (Yukaghir): Nickname for Nikolay Likhachev. The oldest living Yukaghir, he began an apprenticeship as a shaman but was stopped by the Communists.

IGOR KOLOMETS: The author's occasional nickname among the hunters and his pseudonym when he wrote articles for the Yakutsk-based newspaper *Ilken*.

ANATOLIY MAKSIMOV (Sakha): Former vice president of
Sakhabult. He drowned under mysterious circumstances when
attempting to establish the competing fur corporation Bulchut.

MIKHAIL NIKOLAYEV: Former president of the Republic of Sakha
(Yakutia).

NIKIFOR PETROV (Sakha): President of the Yakutian state-
supported fur corporation, Sakhabult. He is related to former
president of Yakutia Mikhail Nikolayev.

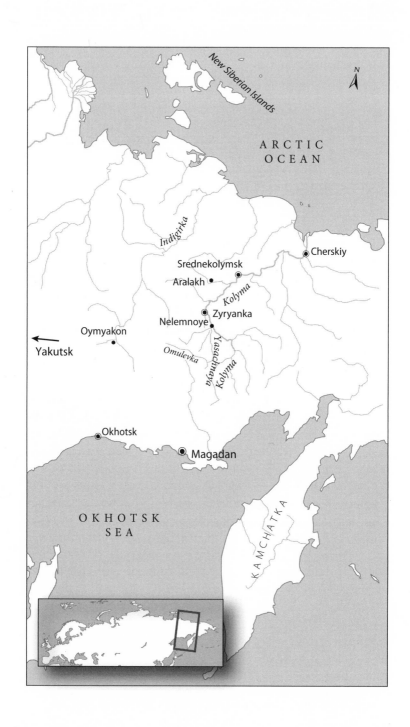

New Siberian Islands

ARCTIC
OCEAN

Indigirka

Cherskiy

Srednekolymsk
Aralakh

Kolyma

Zyryanka
Nelemnoye

Oymyakon

Yakutsk

Omulevka

Yasachnaya

Kolyma

Okhotsk

Magadan

KAMCHATKA

OKHOTSK
SEA

ONE LAST, FEEBLE ATTEMPT

I run my fingers down over my face. My cheeks are hollow, and my eyes feel as if they are sinking into my head. After a week without any food at all, I no longer feel the hunger gnawing at my stomach. But my physical strength has been used up long ago. My arms, my chest, and my legs, my entire body is weakened from exhaustion. Every movement takes such an effort that it feels as if I am stuck in a vise. I know it will not be long before I am too weak to hunt. And then we are finished.

Ivan is lying rolled up in his sleeping bag on the wooden bunk across from me. He is breathing faintly. Then he is quiet. Is he dead? I listen. No, he is still breathing. Ivan is more severely weakened than I am. He has suffered frostbite in his right foot and can no longer walk.

I stare at the empty tin can on the little wooden table where we have put the last of our stock of ammunition. Four cartridges are all that is left. I am overwhelmed by a feeling of utter hopelessness.

"How the hell are we going to make it?" I open the cabin door and step outside. The murderous frost immediately makes my lungs contract and my face stiffen like a mask. I pull my wolverine fur cap down around my head and cast a glance out at the taiga, the naked, deserted forest.

"What the hell are we going to do?" We have no food and have not seen the shadow of a moose for more than a month. Somewhere in the winter-clad taiga, not far from the cabin, a hungry rogue bear is wandering restlessly about, ready to fall upon us.

Map of northeastern Siberia. Drawing by Louise Hilmar.   1

Yura and the other hunters who were supposed to meet us several weeks ago never showed up. The leader of the Yukaghirs has disappeared with the three hundred sable furs we collected, and the police in Zyryanka have issued an arrest warrant for me.

"What the hell are we going to do? . . . What the hell are we going to do?" I repeat to myself, as if my voice is the only thing keeping me from losing control and falling flat on my back from exhaustion and despair.

Ivan and I are caught in the taiga—the huge forest area stretching in a broad band across Siberia, from the Ural Mountains in the west to the Bering Sea in the east, and from the Mongolian steppe in the south to the Arctic Ocean in the north, an area of roughly 4.5 million square miles. There are places here where no human has ever set foot. In reality, this wilderness is the limit to the distribution of human life. With temperatures that can drop to minus 97 degrees Fahrenheit in January, this is the coldest place in the world that is inhabited—albeit sparsely—by people. The cold cuts like a knife through fur clothes and hoods, and just breathing in the air is painful. The ground is always frozen solid, covered by a three-thousand-foot-thick cap of permafrost in which fossilized mammoths, woolly rhinoceroses, bison, and other ice-age giants lie hidden away.

The people who live in this vast, harsh wilderness rely largely on hunting for a living. But hunting is a game of chance; luck counts just as much as experience. One day, you might win: your prey comes running toward you as if voluntarily sacrificing its own life so you can go on living. But at other times, the quarry seems to have vanished from the face of the earth and cannot be tracked down. When this happens, hunger sets in—a hunger that drains you both physically and spiritually and leads only one place: death.

"Can we make our way back to Nelemnoye?" I think to myself.

Compared to the enormous dimensions of the taiga, the village we came from is just around the corner, but in these parts that means roughly 125 miles through unfamiliar and uninhabited terrain. The thought of making it there on foot crosses my mind only briefly before I realize the hopelessness of the plan. Ivan would never make the journey on his injured foot.

And even if we made it to the village, I would be at the mercy of the police waiting for me. At best, I would end up in a Russian prison in Yakutsk, where the tuberculosis would kill me sooner or later. At worst, the police would kill me before I even made it out of the Zyryanka jailhouse.

I collapse onto the chopping block next to Jack and Bim, who lie watching me with dull eyes. They also seem to have given up hope. They are the last dogs we have left. The rest have been knocked on the head and used as dog food. How did I end up sitting here in the Siberian taiga, starving to death? How could I be so naive as to think I could reverse Siberia's entire history of brutal and ruthless exploitation of the indigenous trappers?

In hindsight, the fur project seems not just foolhardy but a downright senseless initiative taken by naive Europeans without the faintest idea of the realities of post-Communist Russia. This is a country that within a few years has turned from a superpower into pure anarchy. Trade has collapsed. The ruble has lost its purchasing power. Organized crime has infiltrated every aspect of society. The law is no longer a question of what has been passed in parliament and is written in the statues, but about who has the power and the means to steamroller their own agenda through. As a political commentator expressed it, "Russia is a country ruled by men, not by laws."[1] One might add that these men are often the most repulsive types, the same people who were good at manipulating the Communist system.

And I wonder how Uffe is doing, my old friend and partner in the fur project. He is probably in Denmark, but what will happen to him once the sable furs fail to arrive at the auction back in Glostrup? He will be unable to repay the thousands of Danish kroner he borrowed from an Arab businessman in order to launch the fur project. Perhaps Uffe is also trapped in a hopeless situation. In any case, the Arab businessman did not seem like the type to readily accept a financial loss.

In this all-embracing hopelessness, I make a decision. I get up, walk into the cabin, put the last four cartridges in my pocket, pull the carbine down off its nail by the door, and set off into the silent, frost-stiffened landscape. This is my last, feeble attempt to force life out of the taiga before it takes ours.

THE FUR PROJECT

1

SHALUGIN, LEADER OF THE YUKAGHIRS

KOLYA SHALUGIN wears an old navy suit with broad, dark stripes. The material is smooth and shiny and has a metallic glint in the midday sun when he steps out of the transit area in Kastrup airport in Denmark to meet Uffe and me. As he stands there in the throng of stylish businessmen and relaxed holiday guests, Shalugin in his suit looks like a curiosity from a bygone era. But he wears it with pride: this was the uniform the powerful bureaucrats wore when they left the office buildings of the state farm to pay the hunters a visit. And the Soviet party leaders wore suits like this when they stood waving on the balcony at the annual military parade on Red Square that was broadcast on television.

For Shalugin, the dark suit is, in other words, the symbol of power and decisiveness, and this is exactly what he wishes to express that morning in July 1994. But the clean cut of the suit does not quite fit his short, stout figure and broad facial features. His hands are dark from the unfiltered sun and wrinkled from frost—a testimony to his past as a trapper. They keep a tight, nervous grip on his suitcase. But above all else, Shalugin's restless body stands in stark contrast to the cool, formal facade of the suit. He never quite stands still; if his body comes to rest for a brief moment, then his little pointy, pouting mouth begins to move in and out.

"Come on, Dusha, Rane is over there." His wife, Dusha, walks

PREVIOUS: Yura Spiridonov aiming a rifle, with Slava Sinitskiy behind him.
FACING: A Yukaghir hunter shows his catch of sable pelts.

behind him with short, excited steps. She drags their teenage daughter, Alesha, by the arm, pointing enthusiastically at the many radiant shops and cafés in the airport.

Shalugin and I know each other well after my visit to the village of Nelemnoye during the film expedition the year before. But this is his first encounter with Uffe and Copenhagen, and Shalugin is clearly nervous. He feels in the big city the same way he feels in his suit—like a stranger. After the various formalities have been exchanged, we guide Shalugin, his wife, and their daughter into an airport café. Shalugin drinks one cup of coffee after the other, chatters loudly, and gesticulates nervously. He has loosened his thin tie and is sweating a little.

"There have been many obstacles. Many evil wills have tried to keep us apart, but now we have finally succeeded," he proclaims.

The meeting has been planned for a long time. Uffe and I see it as the first breakthrough. The first meeting between the representative of the hunters and the Western fur market. We have almost begun to believe that the project we started several months ago will finally succeed. If all goes well, the Yukaghir hunters will soon have the opportunity to sell their sable furs without middlemen at the Danish fur auction.

"Of course, it has been a long trip, and you must be tired. Let's talk business tomorrow," Uffe says kindly, nodding understandingly to Shalugin. But Shalugin does not understand and instead takes the words as a challenge.

"Tired? Mr. Christensen, I am not tired as long as the sun is out." Shalugin laughs loudly, showing his toothless upper jaw. He speaks incoherently and continuously in broken Russian. "My hunters are ready now. They know where their interests will be best served. Here among our Danish comrades and business partners. I myself hunted twelve sables in one day. If I keep it up, I can almost be your fur supplier single-handedly."

Shalugin laughs again. His wife, Dusha, sits proudly listening to her husband's monologue, smiling as she puts away one pastry after the other. Alesha stares hypnotically at a TV screen above the table, where commercials are playing silently. She has tight plaits, tied up with red nylon ribbons, just like the pioneer corps of young Communist girls in the old Soviet Union. Shalugin tells us about the many times he has flown to Yakutsk to discuss his big economic plans with the officials of the republic. He expects to fly even more now that the trade connections are in order, he says as he orders a new cup of coffee, which he drinks with the same nervous, hectic movements as the previous one.

Shalugin under Pressure

The Yukaghirs' primary source of income is the sable, or *Martes zibellina* as it is called in Latin. The sable belongs to the weasel family and is no more than twenty inches long, including the tail. The animal lives only in Siberia and northern Mongolia and China, where, because of the severe cold, it develops a special soft and silky coat that varies in color from light brown to black.[1] The most prized sable fur is blue-black with scattered silver hairs and is known as "black diamond."

Since the very beginning of Russia's expansion beyond the Urals, fur has been one of the most valuable items of trade, and for the indigenous peoples of Siberia it is still the main contribution to the Russian economy. However, although the Soviet government from the outset abolished the much hated fur tax that used to be paid by the indigenous peoples to the czar as a token of their political subjugation, in reality the Communist rulers were no less inclined to make the colonial natives pay for the privilege of being ruled by the Russians. The Soviets introduced a trading system whereby the Siberian natives supplied sable furs through state procurement agencies, receiving a fixed low price in exchange, with which they could purchase basics, such as flour, tea, sugar, gasoline, ammunition, and traps. The furs were then sold by the state at the international auctions for millions of dollars, thus providing the Communist government with an important flow of foreign currency. So, within the Soviet state, the indigenous hunters performed the same function as they had under the czars, providing profit for their "masters" by hunting and trapping fur-bearing animals.

The situation after the collapse of Communism is no better; in fact it is much worse. Now it is the Yakutian state enterprise, Sakhabult, that is controlling the fur trade. The hunters' furs are still being collected for a fixed low price, but virtually no state-subsidized commodities are delivered in return. Sakhabult is taking all the profit from the fur trade in a spirit of idiosyncratic Yakutian nationalism.

At a stroke, it has become extremely tough to live as a Yukaghir hunter at the periphery of the former Soviet Union, and Shalugin feels the pressure from the collapsing economy every day. The hunters back in Nelemnoye have given him the nickname "Choo-Choo" because he moves like a train that is constantly late. His short, stocky body moves laboriously from one place to the other without ever pausing. There is something mechanical about his unrest. Like an old, chugging Soviet locomotive, he rumbles along. One moment he is standing in front of you, and the next he is on his way. He has a kind of mobility that once gave him power as leader of the *obshchina* "Teki Odulok," a commune that represents the Yukaghir hunters in their dealings with the Yakutian central administration and Sakhabult in Yakutsk. However, Shalugin's hypermobility also indicates an unreliability that is devouring the organization from within. Both economically and politically, the *obshchina* has strayed out into an economic storm. It has no revenues and so cannot supply gasoline, ammunition, or anything else the hunters need to go hunting. The setting of prices on foodstuffs is no longer a political question. The price of things is now determined not by the state but by the free market. A barrel of gasoline costs the equivalent of two hundred dollars, where it had previously cost five. Supplies of gasoline, weapons, and foodstuffs are no longer as natural as nightfall. But the Yukaghir hunters do not understand the new situation. They expect Shalugin to provide all the gasoline and all the gunpowder they need, just like the state farm did during the Soviet era. They take it for granted that they will get everything they ask for. Shalugin's popularity rests on this expectation among the hunters. As a last-ditch effort to maintain his status, Shalugin has begun to sell off vehicles and other valuable technology that was allocated to the *obshchina* when the state farm was dissolved, and then to distribute the money among the hunters. To keep his never-stationary train going, Shalugin has begun to use the *obshchina's* fixtures and fittings as fuel. If he goes on like this, the whole organization will soon be burned up.

Copenhagen Is Expensive

The drive to Copenhagen is just as confusing and hectic as the visit to the café in Kastrup Airport. Shalugin is still talking profusely and rapidly. Uffe and I try to tell him of our plans and thoughts for his visit, but Shalugin is too enchanted, too fascinated by the many cars, by the landscape, which is covered with asphalt instead of frost, by the high and densely packed brick buildings. He feels that he has to live up to the power and strength the city displays, so the whole way from the airport to Copenhagen he takes the initiative to tell us about his hunting achievements, his political powers, and his raw strength.

"My father was a good hunter, and his father was a good hunter. But I am also a good businessman," says Shalugin, staring insistently into Uffe's eyes.

Shalugin and his wife and daughter are given lodgings in an apartment in the center of Copenhagen. The apartment belongs to the film producer Thomas Sonne, who took part in our expedition to the Kolyma region. Sonne filmed the expedition and was, like my brother and myself, deeply affected by our meeting with the Yukaghirs. They received us with immense hospitality and warmth, which is typical for a hunting people. Also, they saw us as a sign of a new and better time to come, which made the meeting with them even more charged.

My twin brother, Eske, and I are still poor students at this point, and Sonne is the only one who has a job with a fixed salary, so it is only fair that he takes the task of putting Shalugin up. Sonne takes his assignment very seriously. He wants to show Shalugin that we are grateful for the Yukaghirs' hospitality, so he puts a wad of thousand-crown banknotes in a drawer so that Shalugin and his wife can buy food and drink for themselves for the duration of their stay.

But the money is quickly used for a lot of other things. Each day, when Sonne comes home from work, they have supplied themselves with salmon, hares, and large quantities of clothes and makeup. Several times he sees Shalugin come strolling along from a specialty butcher's with a whole skinned hare dangling under his arm. Dusha has got new dresses in all kinds of colors. They lie spread out across the bedroom, so that it looks like a psychedelic art installation in pastel colors. The rest of the apartment is overflowing with chocolate boxes, soda bottles, and toffee wrappers.

"Sonne, my son, Copenhagen is expensive," says Shalugin one day, when Sonne pops by the apartment.

"Yes, I can see that from all these things," replies Sonne, putting a new wad of banknotes in the drawer. It is only because Sonne genuinely believes that our fur project can create a better life for the poor hunters in Siberia that he keeps on sponsoring Shalugin and his family. Otherwise his patience would long since have run out.

Within a few days of the family's arrival, Shalugin, aided by his wife, has squandered a small fortune, not because Shalugin wants to exploit Sonne's hospitality, but because Shalugin follows a hunter's logic. Sonne has plenty, Shalugin thinks, so he has to share. By sharing, the community of hunters has survived for many thousands of years under the harsh conditions of Siberia. Not everybody can have the hunting luck on his side, but the hunter who has must obviously share his spoils. Shalugin does not understand, however, that Sonne cannot keep on fetching new money when the old is spent. He cannot understand that resources are not infinite, that they do not reproduce themselves as in nature.

However, Shalugin wants to show some gratitude for Sonne's generosity. After a couple of days when Shalugin has had a chance to experience Denmark's fickle summer weather with clouds and rain, he goes to the local hardware store one morning and buys a stack of saws and a couple of axes.

"Now we have to get ready for winter," he says when Sonne stops by later, and before he has a chance to inquire more closely into what exactly Shalugin has in mind, he is dragged out the door and down to the street. Shalugin has long noticed that Rosenborg Castle Gardens—a park in Copenhagen city center, adjacent to one of the royal palaces—has some massive trees whose branches reach high up into the heavens. In a serious tone, Sonne explains to Shalugin that he will be put in prison and later thrown out of the country if he starts to hack away at trees with his ax, and Shalugin throws the ax away and abandons the project.

One afternoon, my girlfriend, Ida, is out for a walk with Dusha in a large public park north of Copenhagen, formerly a royal hunting ground, called Dyrehaven. Dusha has by this time been living in the city center for a while, so the woodlands and the free-ranging deer provide a little diversion for her. But the animals surprise her.

"They can be eaten," she says, pointing to them, amazed that nobody has yet shot them. The cultivated natural area is a mystery to Dusha. But she is the first to understand that the free-ranging animals are just an expression of Danish affluence. Here we have so much that we can afford to let good quarry walk past unheeded. Dusha sees the free-ranging animals as a demonstration of power. She is perhaps the member of the Shalugin family who best understands the world that they have been cast into.

Shalugin has begun to see his Danish hosts as part of the family. He calls Sonne and me his "Danish sons." He begins to behave like a father, like a patriarch who will ensure that Sonne does not freeze when it turns cold. But like a patriarch, he also begins to demand respect. Suddenly, Sonne, Uffe, and I are committed. Among the Yukaghirs it is difficult to deny one's family anything. For this reason, it is also very difficult for us to disagree with Shalugin. If he does not get the influence and attention that a patriarch deserves, he behaves like a domestic tyrant who had been humiliated in his own home. He is quick to anger and sits in a corner sulking if things do not go his way.

Pragmatic Christianity

"You are to be my godfather," Shalugin tells me one afternoon when he has been out for a walk with Dusha and their daughter.

Having bumped into a minister from the Church of Our Lady in Copenhagen, Shalugin wants to have himself and his family baptized. My girlfriend, Ida, and I are to be godfather and godmother. Shalugin insists. Without further consideration, Shalugin and his family are baptized. Shalugin wants to partake of everything he sees around him: the affluence, the security, the stability. He must be possessed by the spirit, whoever it is, that is responsible for the Danish people and their wealth.

Like all other Yukaghirs, Shalugin has a very tangible and practical relationship to religion. Shalugin's gods are hunting spirits. It is they who determine whether he has luck when he hunts. It is they who determine whether he is to starve or to stuff himself with juicy meat. So, naturally enough, Shalugin fills his baggage not just with clothes and CD players but also with Danish Christianity, in the hope that it will help him to partake of the wealth he has experienced since he came to Copenhagen.

The Yukaghirs' encounter with Christianity is, however, nothing new and actually goes back to the conquest of Siberia. But the first time round, the conversion of the indigenous population was a somewhat sickly affair, as the Russian state had a vital economic interest in keeping the indigenous hunters as pagans. The tax category you belonged to was determined by your religious affiliation: if you were Orthodox Christian, you were categorized as *promyshlenniki* and had to pay a royal tribute of 10 percent. If, on the other hand, you were a pagan (Russian, *inoveretes*), you were categorized as a "foreigner" (Russian, *inozemets*) and had to pay *yasak*. As the *yasak* was much higher than what the Christian Russians paid in tax, there was an obvious advantage for the state to keep as many pagans as possible, and so it opposed every comprehensive kind of missionary activity. The only ones the state wished to convert were the indigenous women, so that they could marry the newly arrived Cossacks.[2] Seen in this light, it is perhaps not surprising that the first Russian missionaries who were sent to Siberia to convert the pagan indigenous peoples were usually bankrupt and drunken priests who had either been expelled from their churches or forced to abandon their vocations. Often it was the priests who converted to the hunters' spirits, and not the hunters who converted to Our Lord.

A special group of Christians who traveled to Siberia were known as the "Old Believers," or schismatics (Russian, *Raskolniki*) as they were officially called. They refused to follow the reforms and innovations that the Russian Orthodox Church underwent in the middle of the seventeenth century, and stubbornly went on practicing the old Christian customs and rituals despite their brutal persecution by the government. There was even a program to persecute them. The line was that all schismatics who did not renounce their heresy after third-degree torture were to be burnt at the stake. Often, however, the Old Believers themselves chose to commit mass suicide by assembling in their houses or in a monastery and allowing themselves to be burnt when the government's troops approached.[3] At the end of the seventeenth century, the persecutions quieted down a bit, and the Old Believers were invited to emigrate to Siberia, where they could create a new future for themselves. They settled down primarily in the southeast corner of Siberia, around Lake Baikal, where they can still be recognized by their old-fashioned clothes and dialect.

Another banished religious group were known as *Skoptsiy*, "the Castrated." They regarded sexual abstinence as the way to divine salvation, and to ensure that the ban was observed, they castrated their male members and cut the breasts off the females. *Skoptsiy* settled primarily near the River Lena, in the areas around Olekminsk, in Yakutia. Today—not surprisingly—there are no living descendants of the sect, nor did they apparently have much luck in converting the local Sakha, who, the Russian anthropologist Waldemar Jochelson writes, are all too fond of eroticism to be converted. If we are to believe Jochelson, they only managed to convert a single Sakha to the sect, and he was paid a considerable sum of money to submit to the ritual castration.[4]

It was not until the beginning of the eighteenth century, under Peter the Great, that missionary activity seriously got under way in Siberia. He wanted to modernize Russian society according to a Western European model, and this involved a certain standard of civilization. The population in a modern nation, which Russia was to become, could no longer be pagans. So while the Russians were to be made into Europeans, the Siberian indigenous peoples were to be made into Russians, and conversion to the Orthodox faith was still the way to do it. In 1702, Peter the Great sent a crusade of missionaries off to Siberia with instructions to "find their seductive god-idols and burn them." If the indigenous people resisted, they were to be put to death.[5] But the official rhetoric was one thing, and reality among the missionaries was another. They did indeed succeed in baptizing thousands of indigenous people, including Yukaghirs. But it could only be done by bribing them with gifts or liquor or by temporarily relieving them of their obligations to pay *yasak*.

The Swedish explorer Friherre A. E. Nordenskiöld describes a baroque baptismal ceremony among the Chukchi, who are a neighboring people of the Yukaghirs. On the promise of a few pounds of tobacco, a young Chukchi consented to be baptized. According to the ritual precepts of the Russian Orthodox Church, the body of the "child" being baptized must be dipped in the water a full three times. The young Chukchi jumped bravely down into the tub of cold water but came up again just as quickly and, shivering with the cold, shouted, "My tobacco! Give me my tobacco!" The priest made persistent attempts to explain to him that the ceremony was far from over and that he was obliged to jump down into the bath twice more. But his sermon fell on deaf ears. The Chukchi jumped around with chattering teeth, constantly shouting, "It is enough! Give me my tobacco!"[6]

This story is a brilliant example of the terribly pragmatic relationship to Christianity that prevails among many indigenous peoples in Siberia. In recent times, I have seen a few Yukaghirs wearing brass crucifixes around their necks, but I am quite sure that hardly any of them have a clear idea of what the cross means. Most regard it as another amulet for their protection.

The same kind of utilitarian thinking applies during Shalugin's baptism. The baptism ceremony becomes a major event, which attracts not only many churchgoers but also journalists from the national newspapers. The minister is determined that Shalugin and his family enter into the Christian faith in the best possible way. Shalugin has told him that he has plans to collect money for a church in Nelemnoye, an idea that appeals strongly to the minister in the Church of Our Lady. So he starts a collection among the congregation. During the baptism itself, contrary to the customs of the Danish national church, those present are invited to contribute to the forthcoming church in Siberia.

Throughout the entire proceedings, I am not sure how to respond. I am well aware that Shalugin most likely has no intention of spending the congregation's money on a church. On the other hand, I know perfectly well that if I expose him, Shalugin will never speak to me again, and the whole fur project will go down the drain.

Part of the Family

With the baptism, Shalugin and I come into direct kinship, and in Shalugin's eyes I become the man who will function as the intermediary between him and Denmark's wealth. Dusha looks forward to taking advantage of this. She is already talking about how her daughter, Alesha, will stay with me while she is studying at Copenhagen University. I am visibly annoyed by her unabashed greed.

But Dusha is not a Yukaghir anyway. She is a Sakha, a member of a people formerly known as the "Yakut." Shalugin is short and temperamental, whereas Dusha is stockily built and reserved—just like the two peoples they represent. She is more cunning, better able to plan for the future, and aware of how to get the most out of her contacts in Denmark. Time after time, she reminds Shalugin of what they are actually entitled to now that they are part of the family. On the other hand, she also understands the principles of the Danish–Yukaghir Fur Project and that it is necessary to give something back. Shalugin cannot just draw resources out of Copenhagen. Something must also be provided for the money: first and foremost cooperation and willingness on their part and ultimately what the project is all about, namely, sable furs.

It is also Dusha who gets Shalugin to take the meeting seriously when they tour the Danish fur auctions in Glostrup, Kopenhagen Fur, a few days after their baptism. Shalugin is to meet his hunters' future trading partners. Along with Uffe, he and Dusha are introduced to the directors of the auction and learn how everything will run when the trade partnership is set up. They are led around the rooms at "the Fur," as the auction house is also called. Shalugin is impressed. There are tons of furs hanging on hooks in long rows everywhere. The sight leaves him both moved and elated. The baptism has given Shalugin a self-confidence and an affiliation with the Danish reality.

"This, my friends, is the start of a long partnership that will benefit both of us—a long friendship between two peoples," he proclaims ceremoniously after the tour when they have settled into the restaurant in the Fur to eat lunch. The atmosphere is good. Shalugin tells us about the Yukaghirs' hunting traditions, about how competent they are. He promises that there will never be a problem with supply. There is absolutely no reason to be nervous that the hunters may not be able to supply the five hundred sable furs the Fur has set as a minimum.

With great hullabaloo and good humor, the manager of the Fur's department for foreign wild fur, Thomas Rebild, along with his interpreter, Olga Bugge, and Uffe agree to meet Shalugin in Moscow a couple months later. After that, Uffe will go to Nelemnoye and meet the hunters himself, help with the collection and marking of the furs, and function as the *obshchina's* connection to the Fur. The trading connections have been put in place. The collaboration has been set in motion, and the trip to Copenhagen looks like the start of a success.

2

A POST-SOVIET NIGHTMARE

UFFE IS ONE OF THOSE PEOPLE whom I would without hesitation call a calm character. He always encounters problems of any kind with an almost stoical calm. Whether it is because he lived for decades in a remote cabin in the Swedish forest, or because he studied Tibetan Buddhism in his youth, I cannot say. But the fact is that it takes a lot—an awful lot—to worry him. But that day in January 1996, when Uffe steps in through my front door, I can see that his trip to Siberia has been unusually harsh. Not only does he look extraordinarily tired, but his entire forehead is lined with one worried wrinkle on top of another.

"Well, that was an adventure," he says in his own soft, laconic manner. I pour him a cup of coffee. He takes a sip, leans back in his chair, and starts to tell his story. The trip, which should have formalized our fur project, had instead become a grotesque demonstration of the many transition problems of the post-Soviet period.

The problems manifested themselves from the first day. Shalugin had never turned up as agreed. Uffe and the two others from the Fur had sat and waited in the airport in Moscow, where they had planned to meet. For three long hours their only company had been a coffee vending machine and the sound of Russian pop music from a loudspeaker on the ceiling. Uffe had naturally been at a loss. Shalugin was his only link to Yakutsk and the hunters. The whole business adventure seemed to be at an end before it had even begun.

But as usual, Uffe had pulled himself together and had not panicked. Had he not, by chance, been given the phone number to Shalu-

The desolate urban landscape of Zyryanka.

gin's home in Nelemnoye? Paging back and forth in his notebook, he found it and called. The telephone connection to Siberia from Moscow is as unstable as the distribution of everyday goods, but after several patient attempts he succeeded in getting patched through to Nelemnoye.

It was not Shalugin but Dusha who answered: "He's not here. He's in hospital in Moscow. He has never tolerated it, Mr. Christensen. It has always made him sick."

Uffe, who was both surprised and shaken, hesitated a little before enquiring further: "I don't quite understand. What has always made him sick?"

His stay in Moscow had obviously been too intense for Shalugin. While he had been waiting for Uffe, he had visited old friends, and suddenly everything had disintegrated for him. Having vanished without a trace for a month before the meeting, he had now been admitted to the hospital in Moscow with massive alcohol poisoning. Uffe had stood with the phone in his hand and a feeling that all was now lost.

But before he managed to say good-bye, Dusha suddenly announced, "Yegorov, he'll meet you in Yakutsk and send you on to Zyryanka. We're looking forward to your visit." In a few seconds, Dusha had arranged everything.

"I jumped on the plane to Yakutsk, a tad more skeptical with regard to the project than when I had left Copenhagen," Uffe tells me. "But my doubts didn't diminish when we landed at the airport in Yakutsk. The first thing to welcome us was the cold. I must confess, it came as a shock to me. Minus forty-eight degrees cut through my lungs. The transition from the comfortable, air-conditioned airplane to the inhuman frost almost knocked me out. I held my breath for the first couple of hundred paces on Siberian soil." Uffe pauses for a moment and stares intensely at me.

"Can you guess who was waiting for me?"

I shake my head.

"Inside the little house that serves as an arrivals hall for the landing strip stood not just Yegorov, but the manager of Sakhabult, Petrov!"

"Really? What did he want?" I ask.

"I actually don't know," Uffe replies. "But one thing is certain, he was not enthusiastic about our sudden visit. 'Forget it,' he said, when I told him about my business in Siberia. 'The Yukaghirs don't understand business. They are lazy and don't know the value of money. They are a primitive people, Mr. Christensen. No matter how much trouble you go to, they will never understand our world. Anyway, they don't kill more than a few hundred sables. Even if you take what the hunters from the neighboring villages bag too, you won't reach the five hundred furs you need, by far.'

"I smiled politely at Petrov's spiteful warning. I hadn't bloody expected that the competition would be so quick off the mark that he would actually greet me with warnings. But I supposed there was no reason to fall out with him yet, so I let him escort me to the nearest hotel. For the whole taxi ride, Petrov kept coming with a strange mixture of warnings and threats: 'We have our own business and we really have no plans to send our furs to Copenhagen. On the contrary. And if it should ever happen, we'll look after it ourselves. By the way, we have tried to send furs to auction in Montreal, and it didn't go well; the costs were too high and the prices too low, so we prefer to send them to St. Petersburg.'"

Despite the critical Petrov, Uffe nevertheless asked Yegorov to book a seat for him on the next plane to the Yukaghirs' district capital, Zyryanka. From there, Uffe would be able to reach the hunters' village, Nelemnoye. He wanted to meet these hunters for himself— talk to them and hear how they thought they could perform. He was well aware that Petrov and Sakhabult had only one interest: to keep the hunters in their precarious and backward situation so they could go on buying their furs at far below the market price.

"I said goodbye to Thomas and Olga from the Fur, who wanted to travel on south to Irkutsk on fur business," says Uffe. "As for me, I climbed into the little propeller airplane, and after a flight of five to six hours to the northeast, I landed in Zyryanka, where I was to stay for a couple of days."

Uffe interrupts his account, reaches out for his coffee cup, and takes a series of well-earned swigs.

The Ghost Town

I know Zyryanka all too well. It is the last stop before the endless Siberian taiga begins for real. And its outback status is obvious. The first thing that strikes you in Zyryanka is the cold, the silence, and the ever-present decay. All in all, these impressions can have a depressing effect on the new arrival.

Worse, Uffe arrived at the start of January, more precisely in the Russian Christmas vacation period. The Russian Orthodox Church celebrates Christmas ten days later than in Western Europe, so everything is completely closed. The streets are empty, and everything, from buildings to the surrounding landscape, is shrouded in a thick film of frost. It is intense Siberian winter. The landscape looks as if it has been candied. When the sun shines and plays in the snow, it glistens like sweating sugar. The top layer of snow thaws during the day, when the sun is high in the sky, only to become frozen again during the night, when the sun is gone. Subsequently, layer upon layer of almost rock-hard frost deposits itself on everything outdoors. Even the trunks of the trees are wrapped in a thin layer of hardened frost. If your body is not moving all the time, it is in danger of freezing like the rest of the landscape. Movement equals survival in Siberia. A warm and active body is the best protection against the frost. Seen in this light, it is not difficult to understand Shalugin's restless temperament.

But the silence in Zyryanka is not just because the vacation and the winter cold have caused people to withdraw to their houses. Since the collapse of the Soviet Union, the old harbor town has been in decline. When I visited the town for the first time in 1993, the population was about ten thousand. By Uffe's visit a couple of years later, the total has fallen to under three thousand. The Russians have fled back to the areas around Moscow and St. Petersburg. But Zyryanka is a ghost town in more than one sense, as the ghost of Soviet Communism also wanders around in the town's frozen and deserted streets—the result of a brutal ideological project that was supposed to turn the uninhabitable Siberia into a workers' paradise.

■ ■ ■

Under Joseph Stalin, the Central Committee in Moscow decided, as part of the extension of the Soviet Empire, to create an advanced and modern civilization in all parts of the Soviet Union. It was not just the urban proletariat who were to enjoy the fruits of the workers' revolution but also people in the marginal areas.[1] Pioneer towns would be founded everywhere to signal that the future Communist state would not be restrained by anything, even by a merciless and inhuman natural environment. Streets with names like "Third Anniversary of the Revolution" or "Forward" are living reminders of the vision behind the construction. But it was the Soviet Gulag prisoners who paid the price for the impossible project. Thousands of people were sent there to work in the terrible cold. Poorly equipped and undernourished, the camp prisoners died like flies from the cold, hunger, and epidemics in the labor camps around Zyryanka. How many? Nobody knows, because nobody was counting.[2]

It is the bones of these starved prisoners that have laid the foundation for Zyryanka's large apartment complexes, which today constitute colossal mausoleums for the crimes of the Soviet Union. They stand rooted in the rock-hard frost on massive concrete pillars that have been drilled many feet down into the ice. But, with time, even these pillars give in to the permafrost and become crooked, so the buildings now lean at every possible oblique angle. Many of the apartments are still partially full of furniture, as if people had fled in haste from a war or a natural catastrophe that never came.

Incidentally, the extensive camp system is said to have contributed to the fact that Yakutia in general, and the Kolyma region in particular, has become one of the most crime-plagued areas in the former Soviet Union. Instead of going back where they came from after serving their time, many prisoners preferred to stay in the remote backwater, where they could easily resume their shady activities.[3] Today there are reports of extensive organized crime activity in Yakutia, and Zyryanka in particular is infamous for its high murder rate.

During the Soviet era, Zyryanka survived by shipping coal to the rest of the region's towns along the great Kolyma River. The coal came from Ugelna, a mining town a few miles away. Ugelna, which literally means "coal" in Russian, was a symbol of what the Soviet

Union was capable of and was regarded as a wonder of Russian engineering, with its luxury hotels, swimming pools, fitness centers, mud baths, and restaurants. These amenities were all built in the 1960s to attract Russian workers and bureaucrats to the deserted area. After Nikita Khrushchev had exposed Stalin's crimes and dissolved the Gulags, it was no longer forced labor but high wages and privileges that were needed to drive the colonization of Siberia. Row upon row of five-story concrete apartment blocks, popularly known as Khrushchev buildings, were built. Many young Russians saw opportunities there and settled in the town. But Ugelna, like Zyryanka, was transformed into a ghost town in the few years after the collapse of the Soviet Union. Fewer people can afford to burn coal now that the state no longer sets the price. The consumer suddenly has to pay to have the coal shipped hundreds of miles up the Kolyma River, and that is expensive.

Drinking Spree with the Police Chief

Uffe starts to root in his bag. He pulls out a small pile of photos and lays them on the table. I recognize the building right away. It is the only hotel in Zyryanka, a big concrete block where the futuristic murals of the past have gradually been peeled away by the frost.

"I simply had to take some pictures," Uffe says. "The building seemed so symbolic. In the middle of this wilderness of snow and frost is a gigantic, dilapidated hotel. And I was the only guest."

After the first night, Uffe went to have dinner with the mayor of Zyryanka, Nikolay Danilov. He is Shalugin's oldest friend. But in contrast to Shalugin's short, compact body, Uffe had met a tall, well-built man in a big wolfskin coat. When he took his sable fur cap off, a coarse, weathered face appeared. His hair was combed back with Brylcreem, and his eyes were pinched together, even though the lighting was modest in the little café, which is next door to the first private capitalistic enterprise in Zyryanka, a sausage factory. Also sitting around the table were the owner of the sausage factory, Alexander, his wife, and the police chief of the district, the Chechen Ali Irishkhanov, or "Dudayev" as he calls himself, after the legendary air force officer who was the first president of war-torn Chechnya.

Having eaten and chatted a little about hunting and Siberia's new situation, Uffe discovered that Nikolay Danilov's behavior replicated Shalugin's when talk turned to trade. Each time Uffe steered the conversation toward opportunities to implement our fur project, he was fobbed off with a grand speech reminiscent of those that Shalugin used to deliver.

Uffe throws his arms out to imitate Danilov's self-important, pompous manner: "The Yukaghirs survived the forced taxes and starvation of the czarist era. They survived the Sakha's many bloodthirsty attempts to steal their hunting areas. The Yukaghirs will in no time learn to survive the sloppy brutality of the free-market forces, Mr. Christensen. The Yukaghirs are a strong people, and their solidarity will survive everything."

It ultimately made no difference whom Uffe approached; people did not seem to want to talk about whether this fur-trading deal was realistic. He was always met with vacuous, rousing speeches. Was it at all possible for these people to discuss practical issues? Was it at all possible to make an agreement with them and to rely on them to keep their side of the deal? After all, he had made one firm agreement with Shalugin, namely, where and when to meet, and Shalugin had broken it. How was he supposed to get from Zyryanka out to Nelemnoye, where the hunters live?

The questions piled up in Uffe's head, while Nikolay Danilov kept plying him with empty words and Siberian brandy, the vodka that accompanied every meal. They had toasted again and again, first to health, then to friendship, and then to world peace. Then they made a toast to assassinated Swedish Prime Minister Olof Palme. That was Alexander's cunning proposal, because he sensed that it must be impossible for any Scandinavian to refuse that. Finally, when they had run out of excuses, they had toasted—well, just for the sake of toasting.

■　■　■

After a few hours, when everybody had eaten well and drunk heavily, Dudayev invited Uffe home to his house to show him some video recordings from his many hunting adventures. Dudayev lived in a large house with every kind of modern technology, which is very rare in the region. He had his own radio, a video player, and a whole armory of expensive hunting weapons and ordinary handguns. There were hunting trophies both large and small hanging all over the house. He had bagged everything from sables to moose and bears, whose heads now adorned most of the house. For the occasion, his host had had the table laid for a feast of local delicacies in honor of the foreigner. The menu consisted of moose, reindeer, and fish of all shapes and sizes. Everything had been prepared with different kinds of mushrooms and wild herbs.

Uffe was seated on a sofa in front of the TV, and Dudayev put his hunting videos on. The recordings showed Dudayev accompanied by Danilov flying in a helicopter over the taiga, bagging endless game with AK-47 assault rifles. After they had entertained themselves doing that, they landed the helicopter in a place where they lit a gigantic bonfire and held a drinking party. The helicopter and machine guns had belonged to the Soviet state, but in the anarchy of transition, they now belonged to Dudayev. The midlevel managers of the Soviet state had suddenly become the leaders of the new world. All of the many buildings, weapons, and machines they had managed for the state were suddenly ownerless. Dudayev had previously owned nothing, because everything belonged to the state, whereas he now owned everything, and he had not been able to handle the situation. He had taken everything he could lay hands on, and left everything else behind—unguarded.

Dudayev talked excitedly about the hunting as he pointed at the TV screen and poured more vodka for Uffe. In the meantime, Danilov had come by. This provided an opportunity to toast anew. First to health, then to friendship, and before they reached world peace and Olof Palme, Uffe, who is a portly Danish man, had keeled over backwards in his chair and gone out like a light.

"The next morning, I awoke to the sound of a noisy engine," Uffe recounts. "I had a pounding headache and no recollection of how I got home to the hotel. In front of my window was a big, gray, noisy tank, whirling up a dense cloud of smoke. I honestly thought there had been an accident or something. But in front of the smoking tank I saw a grinning Maksim, Shalugin's oldest son. He was the one who was to drive me out to the hunters."

The Vezdekhod tank is the best of the few existing personal tanks in the world, perfect for a climate where there are no roads and where the landscape is covered with ice for most of the year. If it has not been in use for a while, the engine has to be warmed up by lighting a little bonfire under it.

Soon, Uffe was sitting in the tank with Maksim behind the wheel, on their way to the hunters' village. A forest fire had ravaged the area more than ten years earlier, and all across the terrain were charred trees just under the snow cover. The taiga is completely flat, and the burnt-down and reestablished forest and stretches of heath are repeated for mile after mile. For the unaccustomed viewer, there are not many distinguishing features or nuances to set a course by. Only a few lakes and river valleys break the landscape, which lies like a large, uniform carpet of matchstick-thin larch trees, which disappear into the all-consuming horizon.

Uffe had no sense of where they were going. The Vezdekhod worked its way through the snow landscape like an icebreaker, toppling everything in its path. Trees and ice formations were crushed under its caterpillar tracks. Maksim steered the monster like a captain who steers his ship with a compass and his knowledge of the landscape as his only points of reference.

Encounter with Nelemnoye

After a six-hour drive, Uffe could make out the contours of a cluster of small huts standing on the bank of the Yasachnaya River, a tributary of the great Kolyma River. This was Nelemnoye, the Yukaghirs' village. Nelemnoye was formerly a winter settlement, called Nungeden aNil', situated where the Yasachnaya meets the Rassokha River. The Yukaghirs lived a seminomadic life until the 1930s, following the wandering wild reindeer up into the mountains in summer and living in small underground log cabins in Nelemnoye during the winter months. Between 1956 and 1958, the Communist state moved Nelemnoye downriver, about forty-five miles from Zyryanka, and rebuilt it as an actual village, with two-story wooden houses and a coal-fired heating station, in an attempt to make the Yukaghirs settle down. Today the village has a population of about three hundred, of whom half are Yukaghirs and half are Sakha and Russians. Virtually everyone makes a living from hunting. There are no cattle or horses, only a large number of hunting and sled dogs. And indeed the first beings Uffe encountered were East Siberian Laikas, which are shorter and slimmer than Greenland dogs but have the same type of spiral tails. They ran barking after the Vezdekhod. The dogs were irritable because it was feeding time and their last meal had been a whole day earlier. Whining and cranky, they snarled at the Vezdekhod and each other, until a couple of large bowls of stinking, grayish porridge were thrown out in front of them, consisting of boiled-up leftovers and water.

"I myself was a little hungry after the long journey," Uffe recounts. "But the sight and smell of the stinking dog food quelled my appetite. But what preoccupied me most was the question of whom I should contact now that Shalugin was not there? On my way through the wilderness, Maksim had suggested that I go to see Ivan Danilov. He was supposed to have the most beautiful house in the village. Besides, Maksim told me, he was very thrifty, so he always had food. My concern turned out to be completely unfounded."

The Yukaghirs are a hospitable people. If you refuse a guest in these climes, it can mean the death of the visitor, so all Yukaghirs receive strangers with great warmth and generosity. Inside their houses, abundance does not exactly prevail, but when a stranger is invited to table, nothing will be spared. Maksim had hardly turned his big tank before Uffe was welcomed by a small group of hunters, all of whom invited him home to their houses. But when Ivan Danilov turned up, Uffe chose to go with him.

I know Ivan fairly well from my visits to Nelemnoye. He is originally a Sakha, from the village of Aralakh, but settled in Nelemnoye in the 1970s to realize his pioneer dream as an electrician. The management of the state farm in Zyryanka then made him brigade leader and assigned him to keep track of the Yukaghirs: he was to see that they did not get drunk and play cards instead of working. However, Ivan had been fired for asking too many questions about how the state had chosen to organize the Yukaghirs' working conditions.

Now he was trying to start his own sawmill but had not yet succeeded because of the difficult transition from planned economy to free market. The ghost of the Soviet bureaucracy still walks, and private initiatives are literally foreign bodies. But Ivan is, like the Sakha in general, an enterprising man.

At the time just before the Russian Revolution, many travelers described the Sakha's hard-working, dynamic character. "They are the most thrifty, industrious natives in all northern Asia," wrote George Kennan in 1871. "It is a proverbial saying in Siberia, that if you take a Yakut, strip him naked, and set him down in the middle of a great desolate steppe, and then return to that spot at the expiration of a year, you will find him living in a large, comfortable house, surrounded by barns and haystacks, owning herds of horses and cattle, and enjoying himself like a patriarch."[4]

"There is something special about Ivan," says Uffe. "His face is young and open in the same way as his mind. Just on the short walk home to his house, he asked me about everything from Danish politics to the business plans. He was the only person I met who had such a genuine interest in the world. And it seemed as if he thoroughly considered everything I told him. He listened in concentration to my words so as not to miss the slightest point or nuance.

"'Your fur project sounds like a good idea. That's the kind of business our village needs,' Ivan said when I had explained the plans to him and we were on our way into the hall in the beautiful house he himself built. 'Unfortunately, we are completely lacking an ability to plan, here in Nelemnoye. A gift we have got from the Russians, Mr. Christensen. People in the village of Aralakh, where I come from, and which is two hundred miles north of Nelemnoye, have always lived modestly from herding cattle, but when the Bolsheviks came to power, we were forced to raise cattle on an industrial scale. We were to cultivate the land and exploit the potential that Moscow had calculated we were concealing. But just take a look at our deep-frozen soil; there's not much that can grow here—and certainly not grass in large quantities.

"'But there was nothing to do. The Bolsheviks had planned that grass should be grown here, so there was no choice but to sow it year after year, so we could attempt to feed the cattle herd, which never really thrived. We did not reach anywhere near the size of herd they had planned from Moscow. But we were still given resources to breed cattle. The official explanation for the small herd was just that an epidemic had killed the poor animals. Year after year, this mysterious epidemic struck. It is difficult to learn to plan after an education like that.'"

Teething Problems

Before Ivan had managed to say any more about his concerns, a petite lady, about ten years older than Ivan, came to meet them. She had narrow, smiling eyes and very broad facial features. Her black hair was gathered in a long, thick plait that reached down below her waist.

"Welcome, Mr. Christensen. We have been waiting for you for a long time," she said, and showed Uffe into the sitting room, where bread and steaming tea were standing ready.

It was his wife, Alexandra, who is Nelemnoye's doctor. She told Uffe that a bed had already been made for him in the guest room and that he should just say the word if there was anything she could help him with. She turned out to be just as inquisitive as Ivan, constantly asking questions about Uffe's plans for his trip.

"Let's eat first, you can't have a sensible conversation on an empty stomach anyway," Ivan said, kissing Alexandra kindly on the cheek. "After that, I'll bring you out in the taiga to Yura Spiridonov, who is the vice president of the *obshchina*."

"Will I get an opportunity to see the *obshchina*?" Uffe asked, at which Ivan looked at him in amazement and pushed a sheet of paper with a big red stamp on it over to him, saying, "The *obshchina* has never been anything but a stamp, Mr. Christensen. But never underestimate a stamp. Stamps were the unit of currency in the Soviet Union. They determined everything that time, and they still determine a lot."

"What about Sinitskiy, did you meet him?" I ask.

"Yes, I saw both him and his store," Uffe replies. "In fact, he was the one I needed to drive me out into the taiga, where Yura Spiridonov had his camp."

Slava Sinitskiy is as Russian as beetroot salad and vodka and is one of the few people in Nelemnoye who always has gasoline for his snowmobile. He is a head taller than everybody else in the village and has a big head of blond hair. With his wife, he runs the only business in the village, a grocery store. But the grocer has run into a minor crisis. After the collapse of the Soviet Union, the state no longer transports everyday necessities to Siberia, and private transport costs are so high that it is not viable. So the store is virtually empty of goods, yet all the shelves are still there, and it opens every morning at eight. A couple of cans of pickled chilies, a little toilet paper, and some bottles of vodka are all that can be bought—that is, if the locals had money to pay with. In the window there are a couple of packs of Russian cigarettes that have obviously been lying there for a long time. The packaging is cracked, and the colors have been bleached in the sun.

"When Ivan and I came into the store, Sinitskiy's wife was standing at the counter," Uffe recounts. "She was wearing the typical Soviet grocer's uniform, a long white coat and a hairnet that covered her big red curls. Even though the store didn't have a lot of goods to offer, I think she stands there every single day in her uniform. 'Ivan!' a voice came from the back room of the store. 'You are arriving just as we were talking about you. For the first time in a long time we have had lots of visitors in the store today, but not one has bought anything. On the other hand, all of them have told the same story, that a European has come to the village.' It was Sinitskiy who came out into the store, smiling, and greeted me enthusiastically. 'And it was about time the outside world paid a bit of attention to our little village,' he said."

Uffe continues: "Sinitskiy had already gotten his snowmobile ready, so we could get out to Yura Spiridonov's camp. Sinitskiy was well aware of what my business was, and he also knew that he was the only one with gasoline in his snowmobile. Apparently that's how it is in the village. Everybody knows what their role is, and so Sinitskiy is the man with the gasoline. Before long, Ivan, Sinitskiy, and I were sitting on a snowmobile with accompanying sled, traveling at high speed. Yura Spiridonov's camp was not impressive. In fact it consisted solely of a simple canvas tent with a rusty metal stove. Yura himself is a short but muscular man with strong, broad hands after many years of much too heavy physical labor. He was sitting skinning a sable when we arrived, and I immediately noticed that the fur was of high quality.

"But our conversation was fairly brief. 'You should know one thing before you get more involved in this,' he said to me before I had managed to introduce myself. 'Shalugin hasn't drunk for many years, and there is a reason why he has started again. He has buckled, Mr. Christensen. He has sold practically all of the *obshchina*'s machinery, partly to hand out money to the hunters and partly to afford the visit to the fur auction in Denmark. He hoped that his Danish friends would be able to save our future. But when he came home again with the good news, he was met with closed doors and resistance. Sakhabult's management in Yakutsk immediately started to promise our hunters more gasoline and vodka when they heard about his trip to Denmark. Our hunters always take what they can get here and now—not what is to come. The truth is, Mr. Christensen, it's not just Sakhabult that does not want our business to succeed. It's much greater forces. Forces so big that they have gotten Shalugin to drink himself half to death.'"

Yura had poured vodka for Uffe, Sinitskiy, and Ivan by the open fire. However, he did not drink any himself.

"I haven't touched booze for ten years and I'm not starting now. It almost destroyed me," he explained to Uffe. "Ivan and Sinitskiy can drive you back to Nelemnoye when the sun rises, but go back to Zyryanka tomorrow, because Shalugin is coming back in a few days." That was the last Yura said before he lay down in the tent.

"That put my mind at ease," explains Uffe. "I was convinced that Shalugin had now recovered and that he would come home to resume the negotiations. So the next morning I went with Ivan and Sinitskiy back to Zyryanka, again hoping to get a deal in place."

Shalugin's Fall

But in Zyryanka, Uffe got a bit of a surprise. Some days afterward, a helicopter arrived, and sure enough Shalugin was on board. But out of the helicopter came four big men in suits with little Shalugin completely pinned between them. He was the only one who did not have a suit on, and that had clearly affected him. In a brief glimpse, Uffe saw how Shalugin hung his head before he disappeared behind the tall men, who sullenly led him into the hotel. This was the Yakutian legal state in action. Shalugin had been indicted for having sold all the machinery that was allocated to the *obshchina* after the collapse of Soviet rule. In the course of a few days, Zyryanka had become populated with Yakutian bureaucrats and officials, who all stayed at the same hotel as Uffe.

I look in shock at Uffe, who nods in affirmation and continues his account.

"Well, I tried a couple of times to get in contact with Shalugin, but it was impossible. He was constantly escorted by the four broad-shouldered men, and was under house arrest in the hotel. In the end I gave up and came home to Denmark. The morning after I got home, I received a call from Ivan. He told me that Shalugin had been acquitted. 'They simply couldn't find any motive, Mr. Christensen. Those stupid bureaucrats think that everybody thinks like them. They couldn't believe that Shalugin would have shared all the money he had gotten from the sale to the hunters. Bureaucrats educated at the old, socialist party schools and officials who have not been allowed to read anything but Marx and Lenin couldn't believe that anybody could bring themselves to give up material wealth without getting something in return.'"

Ivan had laughed loudly over the phone. On the other hand, Shalugin had been fired as manager of the *obshchina*. Without any evidence, the only thing the new Russian legal state could do was to ensure that Shalugin was never given official influence again.

3

ONE DAY IN JULY 1999, I am tramping down the dry, dusty dirt road that serves as the main street of Nelemnoye. Almost three years after Uffe's last visit in 1996, I am back in the village. I was here for the first time during the film expedition in 1993 and have come back twice since then, both times in winter. The fur project is more or less dead since Shalugin's decline, and instead I am visiting the village to continue my field studies of the Yukaghirs and their spiritual culture.

Like a Wild West town, the two-story houses stand peeling and dilapidated on each side of the street, surrounded by scrap heaps of ferroconcrete mesh, beams, rotten furs, and other garbage. In winter the refuse is covered in snow, but in summer it lies exposed on top of the permafrost, which is thawed down to a few inches' depth, and the whole village stinks abominably of urine and kitchen waste. There are virtually no people to be seen. The air is too humid to stay outdoors. Only some poorly dressed children are playing in the middle of the road. They are throwing an empty bottle between themselves and yelling loudly.

The temperature must be about 104 degrees Fahrenheit, and I am completely soaked in sweat. It is strange to think that the difference between the warmest and coldest temperature here is more than 180 degrees. Now I long painfully for the Siberian winter cold. The sun is roasting hot, and around my head swarm hundreds of mosquitoes: abnormally large, long-legged insects with needle-sharp stylets. It feels as if I am shut into a thermos flask full of insects. I have long

A Vezdekhod, a Russian civilian tank.

since given up shaving, because my face is too swollen from the mosquito bites.

Shalugin passes me in the street. He only barely salutes before hurrying on. When I arrived in Nelemnoye a month ago, I stayed in his house. But his wife Dusha's shameless desire for my money got on my nerves, and I decided to move in with Ivan Danilov instead. Shalugin was of course extraordinarily offended, and now he does not speak to me anymore. I cannot help feeling pity for him all the same. After he was dismissed as *obshchina* director, he lost all his influence in Nelemnoye, and worse, people accuse him behind his back of drinking away all of the *obshchina's* money. And who knows whether the powerful chiefs in Zyryanka—the mayor and police chief—also took their slice of the pie.

But despite Shalugin's tendency for corruption, I know that he did not act out of malice but out of a genuine desire to help the hunters to a better life. The problem was just that Shalugin could not handle the task. I myself feel a certain share of the responsibility for Shalugin's sad fate. After all, I was the one who invited him and his family to Copenhagen. Besides, I was at least as intent as he was to start the fur project, which is now in ruins. In more than one way, Shalugin is my guilty conscience.

To succeed Shalugin, the hunters have chosen Slava Shadrin, who is not just the new director of the *obshchina* but also a schoolteacher with a special interest in history and Yukaghir language and culture. I hardly know Shadrin and am a little surprised when he calls me to a meeting at the school. At the main entrance, I pass a white limestone bust of the Yukaghir author "Teki Odulok," or Nikolay Spiridonov, as he was originally called. He is the one the hunters' *obshchina* is named after.

When I visited the school for the first time in 1993, a bust of Lenin stood there, but the Soviet "father figures" have been removed in accordance with the changes in the political climate. Teki Odulok was born into a poor Yukaghir family around the year 1900 but was sent by the Communist Party to Leningrad, where he was educated at the university. Later he had a prominent career as an author, in which he promoted the official rhetoric of the time, that the Soviet state had saved his people from eradication and brought them out of their primitive, ignorant state.[1] In this respect, Teki Odulok is a direct product of Stalin's policy of educating the indigenous population of Siberia, which resulted in the creation of the first indigenous intellectual elite. But tragically enough it was also Stalin who put an end to his life: in the paranoid political climate of the 1930s, Teki Odulok was accused of being a Japanese spy and was executed. It was not until Gorbachev's self-examination process that his name was officially cleared, and today he is a symbol of the Yukaghir struggle for cultural and political independence.

At the school, I ask for Slava Shadrin and am told that he is teaching the children the Yukaghir language but will soon be free. The Yukaghir language has no direct link to other languages.[2] Today it is spoken only by the older generation in the village. For everybody under sixty, the first language is Russian or Sakha. This is chiefly because of the Soviet school system, under which the Yukaghir children were sent away from their parents to boarding school, first in the village of Balygychan in Magadan and later in Zyryanka. There, they were taught exclusively in Russian, and they came back to Nelemnoye without any knowledge of their own language. It was not until the 1980s that Nelemnoye got its own village school, and not until 1986–87 that teaching the Yukaghir language became an official part of the school's curriculum. However, the children virtually never speak Yukaghir with each other but switch over to Russian as soon as they leave the classroom.[3]

A New Start

Shadrin comes to meet me, and we sit in his office. Like Shalugin, he is dressed in suit and tie. But that is virtually the only thing the two men have in common. The contrast between them could not be greater. Shadrin is in his early thirties and educated in the same places as the people who had Shalugin removed from power. Shadrin is not a typical Soviet bureaucrat, but with an education from Russian universities, he knows the language of politics and power. Shalugin was elected because of his personal esteem and charisma, whereas Shadrin is an anemic and reserved man with thick round glasses. Shalugin is extravagant, irresponsible, and colorful, while Shadrin is thrifty and cautious.

Also, it is obvious that Shadrin nurtures a fair amount of mistrust toward me as a European and a foreigner. It is as if he thinks that there must be covert motives behind my interest in the life of the Yukaghirs. Shalugin met us with rousing speeches about fraternity between the hunters and the Danes, while Shadrin greets me with political polemics. With theoretically and ideologically well-formulated arguments, he explains the importance of an autonomous Yukaghir state where the populace decides the laws and where the nation reaps the surplus of nature's fruits. I do not really know how I should react to his monologue, and so I ask casually whether there is any way I can be of assistance. Shadrin is not slow to reply.

"I'd like to take up that fur project you once tried to start with Shalugin. After all, sable fur is the only thing of value here, and if we can get the fur trade with Denmark to work, it will be the first building block in the construction of a Yukaghir state." Shadrin throws his arms out in resignation and continues, "But the problem is that Shalugin left me a totally hollowed-out economy, so we have no money to buy the hunters' sable furs with, and so they are forced to sell them to Sakhabult or on the black market. No bank in Russia will lend money to a Yukaghir *obshchina*. I was wondering whether you might know anybody in Denmark who could lend the *obshchina* around eight thousand dollars. That should be enough to pay out half of the price the furs fetch at the auction in Denmark. After the auction, we will then pay the creditors their money back, and that is of course with a certain return on investment."

At this point, the Danish–Yukaghir Fur Project has been on hold for several years. Uffe and I have actually more or less given up the idea that it will ever be realized. And now Shadrin really wants to revive it. But I wonder whether it is a good idea, seen in relation to all the problems we had the last time with Shalugin. Besides, I have not come to Nelemnoye to conduct fur trading but to research the Yukaghirs' spiritual beliefs. Am I now to spend time and energy on reviving the fur project? And can I trust Shadrin as a partner?

I look inquisitively at Shadrin. Even though he is not a hunter nor particularly impressive in purely physical terms, he has, in contrast to Shalugin, a basic understanding of the hunters' economic circumstances after the fall of Communism. He is a child of the new era. He understands the rules of the game in the new economic situation. In other words, Shadrin knows liberalism's requirement for rational planning, and most important for the implementation of the fur project, he understands that both parties' interests need to be considered if a deal is to be made.

Besides, he is an inveterate idealist and clearly sees the hunters' opportunity to sell their furs on the international market as part of a greater political plan whose actual goal is economic independence from the Yakutian central power, and ultimately also political independence. So Shadrin and I seem to speak the same language.

"I'll see what I can do." I say at last. "I have an idea for a potential sponsor, but I must make a phone call first."

We shake hands, and I go home to Ivan's house. The same evening, I ring Uffe, who is excited that our fur project will be set in motion again. He promises to procure the eight thousand dollars, and he himself will come to Nelemnoye in November to organize the purchase of the hunters' sable furs and to evaluate their expected sale price at the fur auction. Now is the time! More than three hundred years' exploitation of the Siberian hunters will be brought to an end, and the unjust course of history will be diverted forever.

The Greatness and Fall of the Russian Fur Empire

Fur trading is one of the oldest commercial activities in Russia, going all the way back to the Middle Ages.[4] It was not until the conquest of Siberia, however, that Russia gained access to the richest reserve of high-quality fur in the world, namely, the sable.

From the beginning of the conquest in 1500 to around 1700, the export of sable furs was the very backbone of the Russian economy, increasing from 3.8 percent of all state revenues in 1589 to 10 percent in 1644.[5] At that time, the European market was the most important. Many of the forests of western Europe had been felled to make room for agriculture, and most wild animals had been wiped out. At the same time, an expensive fashion trend flourished in Europe, which used fur in great style. In contrast to its European neighbors, Russia possessed an almost endless wilderness east of the Ural Mountains, which was densely packed with sables and other valuable fur animals. The result was that Europe's enormous demand for fur, especially sable, became the driving force behind Russia's conquest of Siberia.

First came the Cossacks, the professional soldiers employed by the state, who built forts and fortified log cabins connecting the newly conquered areas with Moscow and the European fur market. Their conquests gained momentum in 1581 with victory over the Mongol Turkic khanate of Sibir—hence the name Siberia—which had obstructed the Russians' way east of the Urals. Like the rest of the Mongol khanates, Sibir was weakened by internal power struggles, and under the leadership of the legendary Yermak, despite their poor numbers, the Cossacks captured the capital, Kashlyk, and drove Kutchum Khan and his court back to the steppe. With the disappearance of Sibir, there was no longer any significant power to obstruct Russian expansion to the east. In less than seventy years, the Russians conquered the whole of the Siberian territory from the Urals in the west to the Pacific Ocean in the east. The dream of great riches from furs had become reality.

In the wake of the Cossacks came the private hunters and merchants, the *promyshlenniki*. Among them were noblemen, city dwellers, and farmers, all driven by the dream of quick wealth in a "fur rush" that can perhaps best be compared with the Alaskan gold rush.[6] At that point, it was in no way unusual for a hunter to bag between 120 and 280 sables in a season that stretched from the beginning of October to late April.[7] When one considers the sky-high prices of the time, whereby a man could buy a good piece of land with a house in the Moscow area, five horses, ten cows, and twenty sheep for two good sable furs, it is obvious that a hunter could become extremely wealthy in just one hunting season.[8] And this in fact happened for many. The American historian Raymond H. Fisher, who has investigated the significance of the fur trade for Russia's economic development, writes that the Russian fur trade was "the most important single factor in the creation of a comparatively strong and numerically increasing Russian commercial class."[9]

It was not the private hunters and fur traders, however, who dominated the Siberian fur trade, but the Russian state in the form of the czar, who was the greatest merchant in Russia. The czar had three different ways to fill the treasury with fur: taxation, confiscation, and trade. Most important was what was known as *yasak,* from a word common to both Mongols and Turks, meaning "to regulate" or "to fix," which was an obligatory fur tax that was imposed on the indigenous populations of Siberia as they were subjected to Russian supremacy.[10] In fact, the whole colonial administration, its construction of fortresses, its military strategic deployments, its acquisition of new territories, and its categorization of the indigenous peoples into administrative tribes and clans, was guided by the collection of the *yasak.* The fur tax was paid annually by each indigenous hunter or by the clan leader for the whole group. The quantity varied by area and time. In the beginning of the seventeenth century, the taxation was between eighteen and twenty-two sables for each man aged between eighteen and fifty years. *Promyshlenniki* also had to pay a royal tribute of 10 percent to the czar, but the payment from the indigenous hunters constituted most of the state's revenues by far, between 55 and 80 percent.[11]

However, the intense hunting pressure resulted in a constant decline in the number of sables and other fur animals. As hunting territories were exhausted, new ones had to be found, and so the conquest of Siberia continued from one hunting territory to the next until the sable was virtually extinct throughout Siberia. In fact, the sable became so rare after the year 1700 that the fur trade lost its significance as the cornerstone of the Russian economy. Instead, fur from the newly discovered land areas of North America started to dominate the European fur market.[12]

The Soviet Period

Nevertheless, fur started to rebound as an important Russian export during the twentieth century. In 1913, Siberian fur constituted no less than 44 percent of the total quantity of furs sold at the international auctions. Just after the Russian Revolution and the subsequent civil war, when large parts of the industrial apparatus lay in ruins, fur sales accounted for between 10 and 15 percent of the Soviet Union's exports.[13] During this period, the Communist government introduced a series of limiting hunting laws, which led to an increase in populations of sables and other fur animals. At the same time, they released new species of fur animals into nature, for example, the muskrat, which is found in large numbers across the whole of north-eastern Siberia today.[14]

The revival of the fur trade also continued under Stalin in the 1930s and 1940s. In his desire to earn foreign currency for the building of Soviet heavy industry, the system supported the development of intensive trapping. The indigenous communities were organized into "collective farms" (Russian, *kolkhoz*), which were later reorganized into large "state farms" (Russian, *sovkhoz*). Trapping became an industrialized mode of production, designed according to the shift-work system, which was used in other places in the Soviet Union for industrial workers. The state farm equipped the hunters with rifles, traps, and provisions and sent them in brigades out into the wilderness with helicopters.[15] The objective was to reform the market relations that existed in Siberia, under which private traders purchased furs from the local hunters, to a rational, planned economy in which the Soviet state had full control of the fur trade, just as the czar in his time had had.

Under Communism, private trade in fur was not permitted. The hunters had to deliver all their furs to the state farm, which sold them at a fixed low price to the fur exchange in Irkutsk. From there, they were sent on to the international auction in Leningrad (Russian, *Soyuzpushnina*). Eighty percent of all furs were exported and constituted an important source of foreign-currency revenue for the Soviet Union. In the 1970s, the sale of furs accounted for 25 percent of the total exports of the Soviet Union.[16] Instead of direct payment for the furs, the state farm paid the hunters a wage, which was heavily subsidized by the Soviet state. For each ruble the state farm earned from trapping, the state gave an extra subsidy of 70 percent. And indeed the hunters lived well on the scheme, lying in the highest wage category.[17] While the Soviet citizen had an average wage of about 1,200 to 1,440 rubles per annum, an ordinary hunter earned about twice that. The most highly skilled hunters could earn much more, right up to 27,000 rubles per annum. When the low prices of the Soviet era are taken into consideration, where, for example, a plane trip from Yakutsk to Moscow cost only about 100 rubles, it is obvious that a good hunter lived extraordinarily well. So the hunter's wage was nicknamed the "long ruble," because his income stretched very far.

Sakhabult's Monopoly

With the collapse of the Soviet Union in 1991, all of this changed almost overnight. The regional governments were given greater autonomy, and this applied not least to Yakutia, which nationalized all the raw-materials industries, including the fur industry. The president of the republic, Mikhail Nikolayev, declared that Yakutia's laws took precedence over Russia's within Yakutia's territory. This led to the establishment in 1992 of Yakutia's state fur corporation, Sakhabult, meaning "Sakha prey." The corporation trades chiefly in sable fur, and its head, Nikifor Petrov, who is a relative of Nikolayev, quickly monopolized the fur trade in the republic. For this reason it is Sakhabult that purchases all of the Yukaghir hunters' furs.

From its foundation to today, Sakhabult has collected no fewer than thirty-nine thousand sable furs per annum and has had annual revenues of up to $5.7 million, of which sales of sable furs at the international auctions constitute about 66 percent. The total hunting territory under the corporation's control is 188,000 acres, or about 84 percent of Yakutia's combined hunting area. In addition, the corporation owns a large fox farm, a shoe and leather factory, and four fur shops. When the hunters who supply furs to Sakhabult are included, it has a staff in the region of eight thousand. In other words, the firm is a gigantic enterprise.

The principal idea behind the establishment of Sakhabult was not much different from its predecessor, the Soviet state: the hunters were to go on supplying sable furs in exchange for Sakhabult providing gasoline, snowmobiles, ammunition, and provisions. In a special gazette published in 2007 to mark the anniversary of the foundation of Sakhabult, Petrov asserts that the firm supplies Yakutia's hunters with goods and technology to a value approaching twenty million rubles.[18] In reality, the fixed low prices that the organization will pay for the furs are the only thing the hunter is sure of. Sakhabult's agents manage almost never to bring goods or services to the Yukaghirs or other indigenous hunters, and when they do turn up with goods now and again, they are of a poor Chinese brand that cannot be sold anywhere else. They come with leghold traps that do not work, binoculars through which nothing can be seen, or goods that are totally useless to the hunters, such as chili sauce and cans of Coca-Cola that are long past their expiration date. Unlike the Soviet Union, the hunters must now pay the full market price for all of these goods.[19] With a rate of inflation of several hundred percent, the new monopoly system has made the Yukaghirs' hunting economy collapse.[20]

Will our small fur initiative be able to abolish all this misery and injustice and for the first time in Russian history place the Yukaghir hunters in control of the trade of their own sable furs? Our optimism is high when in December, six months after my meeting with Shadrin, we revitalize the Danish–Yukaghir Fur Project.

First and Last Fur Purchase

The first furs are collected when the Siberian winter cold reaches its lowest point. It is 85 degrees below freezing outside. However, at the moment we do not feel the cold much because we are in the home of Nelemnoye's enterprising Sakha Ivan Danilov. His impressive house is as big as a fortress and without doubt the best built in the village. The logs, which are solidly stacked on top of each other to a full three stories, are so finely hewn that not even a sheet of paper can be pushed in between them. Here the freezing wind does not intrude, and no warmth escapes. Even now in winter, one can walk round the rooms in stocking feet.

It has taken Ivan Danilov the best part of ten years to build the house, and he is lacking only a few fixtures and fittings. Parts of the walls are still covered with old newspapers, and a shower closet is also under construction. But the house is already full of furniture, with the familiar bunk and table, but also sofas, armchairs, and curtains with matching colors. For many of the hunters who have never before been in Ivan's house, this is an incredible experience. Just the fact that the floor is not made of rough planks, but covered with carpets, makes them tread carefully.

Behind a big table at the end of the spacious kitchen, Uffe is receiving the hunters and their sable furs. Shadrin is sitting at his right-hand side as a representative for the *obshchina,* while I am sitting to the left, keeping the books. Uffe lifts the pelts one by one and shakes them, so the fur puffs up. He lets his index finger run up along the lustrous guard hairs, painstakingly scrutinizing the different shades of the colors under the light of the desk lamp. He then blows into the hair layer so that the delicate underwool comes into sight, before finally pronouncing his judgment.

"Fine dark and dense fur, but the body length is short and no silver sheen. Twelve hundred rubles now and twelve hundred rubles afterwards."

Half of the expected net sales price of the pelt is paid out straight away to the hunter, while the other half will be paid out after the auction sale. Each pelt is marked with a "talon," or plastic strip with a bar code, that is posted to an account opposite the individual hunter's name. The bar code is proof that the pelt will be put on sale at the Danish fur auctions, and a guarantee that the hunter will receive the rest of the sum when the pelt has been sold. In addition, accounts are kept so the hunters are on an equal footing with professional hunters (Russian, *Kadrovoye okhotniki*), and they are given legal status as cooperative shareholders in the *obshchina*.

It is enormously important for us that the hunters do not just get the price they earn according to market conditions but that they also learn the underlying principles of co-ownership. A hunter is seldom officially registered and is usually not listed as an *obshchina* member either. In other words, he lacks all the legal conditions that are a prerequisite for being able to trade on the free market. That is now being changed. Shadrin has also collected all the permits that are necessary for the *obshchina* to conduct lawful fur trade: the license to store furs, the license to transport furs, and, not least, the license to sell furs. All of the permits have been issued by Russia's Federal Ministry of Agriculture.

Uffe has borrowed the money that is paid out to the hunters from a wealthy Arab in Sweden. So Uffe has given a personal guarantee for the finances of the project—a great risk, as we do not yet know how the whole thing will end. I do not know whether Uffe will be able to pay back the borrowed money—together with the high returns, a total of about eleven thousand dollars—if the project should fail. I dare not ask him. Instead I cross my fingers that the whole thing will succeed. And it really looks like it will.

Word of our fur buying spreads rapidly, and the Yukaghir hunters turn up one after the other to trade with us. Even though our initial cash payment is equivalent to Sakhabult's prices, the hunters are attracted by our promise of an expected bonus of 50 percent after the sale of the pelts at the fur auction.

But the hunters are drawn not just by our money but also by Uffe's personal charm. His calm and confident character has an almost magnetic effect on them. They smile warmly at him, shake his hands, and shower him with compliments: "Thank you, Mr. Christensen, for helping us in this difficult time, may God be with you."

Before long we have gathered 280 sable pelts, which lie in a pile by Ivan's kitchen table. All are of high quality and sparkle in motley colors. But they are not enough. We should preferably have 220 more pelts, since one lot at the auction must by agreement consist of a minimum of 500 hundred pelts. We ask Ivan about the possibility of going to the village of Aralakh, his birthplace, to gather further sable pelts. But Ivan is not optimistic.

"You must understand that Aralakh is not like Nelemnoye. It is a Sakha village. There are very few Russians and no Yukaghirs at all there. The Sakha are nationalistic, and even though they are also being cheated by Sakhabult, they are loyal to the enterprise for the simple reason that it is Yakutian."

Sakha and Yukaghirs

The Sakha, or Yakuts, are the dominant ethnic group in Yakutia, with nearly four hundred thousand people. This is an enormous population in comparison with the Yukaghirs, who consist of only around one thousand. But in contrast to the Yukaghirs, who represent the last remnant of a prehistoric Arctic culture, the Sakha are not originally from northern Siberia. Their ancestors, the Kurykan people, originate from the area around Lake Baikal, close to the Mongolian border, from where they were driven north in the thirteenth century by Genghis Khan's hordes on horseback, who conquered much of the known world and became owners of one of the largest empires in history.[21] The Kurykan themselves advanced along the banks of the River Lena, which at the time were inhabited by Evenki and Yukaghirs and other so-called indigenous peoples. Along the way, the Kurykan painted the cliff faces with images of horses galloping wildly, with riders holding lances or bows or swinging a lasso.[22] It is quite clear that the Sakha's forefathers cultivated horses and the art of riding with great passion. And indeed the Sakha culture of today has maintained distinctive Central Asian features: they are first and foremost cattle- and horse-breeders; they drink fermented mare's milk, koumiss; they speak an ancient Turkic language; and their social organization, in stark contrast to that of the Yukaghirs, is clearly hierarchical.[23]

Traditionally, every Sakha clan has been led by what is known as a *toyon*: an aristocratic military leader who owned large herds of cattle, horses, and slaves and who assembled the clan's free men under his leadership. Marriages were arranged, and women from other clans were bought for a bride price that was set by the families' male members. On the whole, the women did not enjoy particularly high status in Sakha society and were set to carry out the hardest work, such as chopping firewood and mucking out after the domestic animals.[24] All this changed during the collectivization of the 1930s, but the difference between woman and man, rich and poor among the Sakha is still striking.

The Sakha in Aralakh belong to the group known to the Russian anthropologist Waldemar Jochelson as "polar Yakuts."[25] They came to the Kolyma region as a direct result of the Russians' sudden arrival in northeastern Siberia in the middle of the seventeenth century. In the attempt to avoid paying the compulsory fur tax, *yasak,* which the Russian conquerors imposed on them, a group of Sakha fled northwards with their cattle and horses and settled down in the areas around the Arctic Circle. This is the northern limit for herding domestic animals, and so hunting has always been an important sideline for this group of Sakha.

The immigration gave rise to several territorial wars between Sakha and Yukaghirs—wars that the Yukaghirs to a large extent lost because of their small population and lack of unified organization. As a result, the Yukaghirs' territory was reduced during the eighteenth and nineteenth centuries to some scattered enclaves in the Upper and Lower Kolyma regions. Today the bloodshed has long since ceased, but the hatred and mistrust between the two peoples is still going strong. The Sakha generally consider the Yukaghirs to be a primitive, second-class people who are irrational by nature and in-

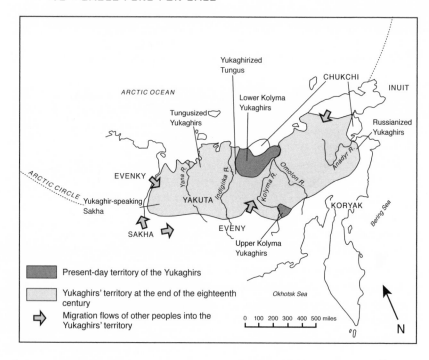

Present-day territory of the Yukaghirs

Yukaghirs' territory at the end of the eighteenth century

Migration flows of other peoples into the Yukaghirs' territory

capable of planning for the future. The Yukaghirs, on the other hand, see the Sakha as selfish and greedy people who refuse to share their wealth with others. This is why a person among the Yukaghirs who displays greed is pejoratively called a "Yakut," a derogatory term for Sakha.[26]

Death Drive to Aralakh

Even though we doubt whether the trip to Aralakh will bear fruit, we nevertheless decide to try. After all, we should ideally have collected more sable furs. But the trip is not exactly straightforward. The drive from Zyryanka to Aralakh traverses about two hundred miles of frost-stiffened and uninhabited terrain. Maybe not that far, but in Siberia, distance is more a matter of accessibility than miles.

We need a Vezdekhod tank, but there is none readily available. Instead we succeed in persuading a local driver named Ayaal to drive us in his Russian "Uazik" jeep. However, he expects to be paid handsomely, since, as he makes clear, "The winter road between Zyryanka and Aralakh is deadly dangerous. If the car breaks down on the way, we are sure to freeze to death."

And cold it has become. The thermometer reads 85 degrees below! Luckily, I am well dressed. My Yukaghir "grandmother" (Russian, *babushka*) in Nelemnoye, whose name is Akulina, has sewn a complete winter outfit for me, consisting of boots and accompanying socks and trousers—all of reindeer fur. For the rest of my

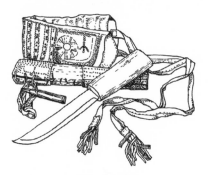

Cartridge belt and knife. Drawing by Sara Heil Jensen.

body, she has sewn a jacket of hare skin, a cap of wolverine fur, and mittens that are finely edged with fox fur, which I can press against my face to warm my frozen-stiff nose and cheeks. In addition, she has embroidered a beautiful cartridge belt. The pearl pattern of the belt represents a kind of magic map with roads and lit-up stars that will ensure that I do not get lost in the taiga.

In contrast, Uffe, who is a stout man, is not dressed for the Siberian winter, and the local clothes are too small for his girth. We solve the problem by dressing him in two coats, one in front and one behind, which are tied together across his chest and stomach with gaffer tape. On his feet he puts a pair of *valenki,* Russian felt boots. It is not ideal clothing but good enough to keep him warm.

Just when we are about to leave the main street in Zyryanka to drive away toward Aralakh, we see a Vezdekhod crawling up alongside us, with a rattling engine noise. It turns out to be Rayon, Sakhabult's agent in the Kolyma region. He is a short, round-shouldered Sakha with a pockmarked face that is almost hidden behind enormous glasses with tinted glass. He stops the tracked vehicle, hops out of the driver's cabin, and walks over to us. He can undoubtedly figure out who we are.

"Well, I hear you're going to Aralakh to collect furs. I am too. Don't expect me to leave any for you." Rayon laughs loudly, revealing an unbroken row of stainless steel teeth. I am intent on documenting all aspects of our trip, so I take my camera out to take a picture of our competitor. A few seconds after the flash goes off, Rayon rushes at me, pulls me out of the car, and swings his fist in front of my nose.

"The next time you photograph me, I'll tear the head off you," he seethes, so close that his spittle hits me in the face. After that, he pushes me away from him, swings up into his Vezdekhod, and roars away out into the silent, frosty landscape.

■　■　■

We realize that we must reach Aralakh before Rayon. Otherwise he will clear the village of sable furs. The advantage of his Vezdekhod is that it can penetrate any kind of wilderness like a knife through soft butter. On the other hand, it is slower than our jeep, if we can keep it driving on the road—or perhaps more correctly on the lack thereof, because after just thirty minutes' driving, the road ends, and we find ourselves on an old forestry path so full of potholes that we are quite literally thrown around in the car and strike our heads on the roof time after time. But the jeep is admirably strong and robust, and seems to be able to handle anything. It is, like all Soviet vehicles, a workhorse, even if a luxury interior and comfortable suspension were not the car manufacturer's highest priority.

Hour after hour we work our way forward through the taiga, steadily being beaten black and blue. Everybody is silent for fear of biting our tongues off if we surrender to careless chatter. Besides, it is perishing cold. The car's windscreen is totally covered in floral ice patterns, so Ayaal has to open the door to be able to keep an eye on the path. The draft freezes me to the marrow, and soon my legs are almost numb, even though I am dressed in reindeer-skin trousers and boots. I look over at Uffe and Ivan, who are also sitting with their teeth chattering.

However, Ayaal does not seem to be particularly bothered by the cold. During the whole drive, he is almost hanging out of the jeep with one foot on the running board and his right hand resting on the steering wheel. Occasionally, we have to get out and push the car free from a snowdrift, and once in a while the engine stops in protest at being pressed so ruthlessly. But Ayaal knows exactly what to do in that situation. First he takes hold of a little Virgin Mary icon, which is dangling in front of the windscreen, and kisses it tenderly to secure the support of the heavenly powers. Next he dashes out of the car, throws the hood up, and takes out an enormous crank handle, which he then uses to turn the engine over. Off we go again, bumping along with the snow spraying along the sides.

"That's it!" Ayaal shouts after more than ten hours of driving, pointing to a short but unusually thick old larch tree standing to the left of the road. Hanging from its many gnarled branches are small, faded silk ribbons and rags, shards of mirrors, cartridges, and cigarette packs. There are a large number of vodka bottles lying beneath the tree. They are all empty, because the spirits have an immense thirst for liquor. Anxious travelers through the centuries have made sacrifices to this tree in the hope that its "owner" will help them safely out of the stiff-frozen taiga.

Ayaal orders us each to sacrifice something of personal value. I give the tree some of my best cigarettes, a pack of Marlboros that I have brought with me from Moscow. Uffe offers some banknotes. When we are sitting in the car again, I ask Ayaal how he can both be a good Christian and at the same time offer gifts to the spirits of the forest. The question seems illogical to him, and he casually answers that he does not see the remotest contradiction between the two things.

"The Virgin Mary helps me out of love, while the spirits help me because they are fond of drinking vodka and smoking cigarettes. If one fails, the other is sure to step in," Ayaal explains.

The Siberian belief in spirits, or animism, is ingenious as a guiding principle for life in the taiga. Even though I have a different attitude at this point, I must admit that I understand the worldview in many respects. Indeed I can almost feel myself tempted by this spiritual psychology. This is a set of beliefs that is in tune with the doings of the Arctic people. It is solely the utility value—that is, what the spiritual powers can do for me—that counts, not woolly messages about mercy and salvation.

Mistrust in the Village

Late in the evening, twenty-four hours after we left Zyryanka, we glimpse the lights of Aralakh between the trees. When we drive down the main street, which is empty of both traffic and people, we see Rayon's Vezdekhod, which is parked in front of the administration building. Ivan spits and throws his arms out in resignation.

"Damn! So he got here before us. Now there is not much hope that we can buy furs," he snarls bitterly.

As for me, I am black-and-blue and beat after the long drive—and annoyed that we have probably arrived too late after all. I look around and am fascinated by the cabins in the village, which are different from the Soviet-built two-story houses I know from Nelemnoye. The Sakha in Aralakh still live mostly in traditional yurts. These buildings are only about six feet high, with a square base and upright poles that lean slightly inwards, so the construction has the shape of a truncated four-sided pyramid. The wooden skeleton of the cabin is covered with larch tree bark, with a mixture of earth and cow manure slapped on. In front of the yurts are tall, meticulously carved hitching posts, often crowned with finely modeled horses' heads, which tradition dictates should be found on every Sakha farm.

Standing against the yurt there is usually a cow stall of the same construction, which is only separated from the human living quarters by a simple wooden door. Now I understand why the Yukaghirs say that a Sakha can always be recognized by his stink of cow manure, because everything in the village smells of cattle. The entrances to both the cabins and the stalls are always oriented toward the west. This is because the Sakha think that the devil, "*Abasy*," brings European disease and other misfortunes from the south. However, *Abasy* has no conception of the past but lives solely in the present. For this reason, he cannot turn around but only go forward. If he should come to a cabin or stall, he will not be able to go in through the door as long as it is not oriented in a southerly direction. Instead he is compelled to crawl up over the roof and continue on his way away from the residents and their cattle.

It turns out that Ivan was right when he said that the people in Aralakh are distrustful of strangers, as the residents observe us only from a distance and apparently do not want contact. Ivan is also ignored, even though he is a Sakha, born in Aralakh. As long as he is in the company of two Europeans like us, nobody will have anything to do with him.

On the street there is a man who shouts something in Sakha to him. Ivan translates it for us: "Take a hike home to the Yukaghirs and take your foreign fur-buyers with you. You're not welcome here." It is obvious that national disposition is valued higher than financial gain here. None of the local hunters is ready to trade with us.

"It's like I said," Ivan grumbles. "There's nothing for us here. Rayon didn't even need to turn the locals against us. They are xenophobic by nature. Let's go over and visit one of my relatives. He is the village veterinarian and the only cultivated person in this damned hole."

Kierkegaard in Siberia

The man Ivan is thinking of goes by the name of Germagen and is a thickset Sakha in his midfifties, with a broad, confidence-inspiring face. He distinguishes himself clearly from the other inhabitants of the village. Even his yurt is a schizophrenic meeting between isolation and education. Along the wall of the earth-sealed sitting room, he has installed a small library, where various classical and European authors are arrayed. Beside the over-filled shelves, which offer everything from Homer and Plato to Kafka and Marx, hang cheap reproductions of photographs representing beautiful, idyllic, and exotic waterfalls and sunsets from warmer climes. Above the fireplace hang portraits of Russian poets and artists—portraits that Germagen himself has painted. In the corner is a traditional horse saddle. I recognize it from the classic ethnographic literature.[27] It is called *Yngyyr* in the Sakha language, and Germagen's model is exceedingly beautiful, decorated with a silver hook and a silver plate in front. The plate of hammered silver is engraved with curvilinear figures and fastened to the wooden frame of the saddle with silver nails. The Sakha horse saddle is heavier and its pommel is higher and rougher than the Mongolian and Buryat ones from southern Siberia. Actually, the saddle of the Sakha is

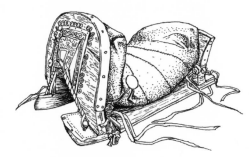

Sakha horse saddle.
Drawing by Sara Heil Jensen.

inconvenient for jumping over barriers, and Germagen assures me that for Europeans, "who are not bowlegged like the Sakha," the breadth of the Sakha pommel causes pain in the hips and groin, making it extremely uncomfortable to sit on.

Our host apparently places greater emphasis on spiritual than physical nourishment, as the only thing he offers us is some canned food and a little vodka. When we have consumed the meager meal, he begins to tell us what a fantastic support the Danish philosopher Søren Kierkegaard's works and thoughts were to him when he was a young student in Moscow.

"With Kierkegaard on my night table, I never felt that I was at the mercy of the Soviet system. Because with him I found out that no matter how restricted my options were, no matter how little control I had over my fate, there was one thing the Soviet state would never be able to take from me, namely, my ability to interpret the course of my own life; to interpret it just as I wished. This is exactly why we as humans are never completely enslaved. It may well be that we all end up in the same place, namely, death. Our Lord has determined that. But how we regard and interpret the course of life that we follow from birth to death, in the end we determine that for ourselves.

"The Soviet system with its deification of logic and reason believed that it could control not just humanity and history but the course of nature itself. In the eyes of the political supervisors, nature was something to be tamed and brought into submission. That was the time when there was talk of diverting the course of the large Siberian rivers to irrigate the agricultural areas to the south. At the same time, the West Siberian tundra began to be looted of its oil. The nuclear power time bomb ticked away cheerfully while radioactive waste was dumped into the Arctic.

"It was believed that the engineer, numbers, and technology could gain power over the soul of nature. But that's an impossibility. There is always something that lies beyond the essence of logic. Not everything in this life can be calculated and categorized. And it is precisely on this point that we are free as humans—the point where our reason, which mistakenly believes that it can predict everything with measuring instruments and computations, breaks down."

■　■　■

The speech makes me think of Ivan's story of how the central administration in Moscow forced the people in Aralakh to intensify their cattle herding, just because its theoretical calculations showed that it would be worthwhile. Even though the experience of the local populace was completely the reverse, it had to be suppressed so that the system would not lose face. The result was that cattle were allowed to die year after year under wretched conditions. In such cases, I suppose it was not actually a matter of reason but of faith—blind faith that the system would be able to conquer all.

Germagen continues: "The Soviet ideologues were so cocksure that they forgot to differentiate clearly between that which is similar and that which is identical. And they tried to develop theoretical models for the world where everything fits together in all directions. They just forgot that all theories are models of reality and not reality itself. In this way, the whole system slid over into a kind of insane state. This is a dangerous tendency that the political has. But Kierkegaard knew that reality lies beyond the word and that we as humans are not capable of coming up with a complete description of the world.

"Only God has a full overview, but he is silent. If the Soviet system had been God, it would with certainty exist today. But it wasn't, since in that case it would have had the power but not the will to rule. Instead the Soviet system had the wish to rule but not the power. Power belongs only to the one who does not want it, who sees it as a necessary evil."

Germagen is without doubt a very well-read and cultured person, and the meeting makes an impression on me. In the middle of this harsh environment, where everything, even religion, is applied and understood in pragmatic terms, sits a mild little man who has adopted the desire for knowledge of intellectual Europe, where knowledge and insight give pleasure, and where satisfaction of one's physical needs are not the guiding principle of existence.

It turns out, however, that Germagen is not pure spirit but also has a more practical side. Before we leave his cabin, he lays on the table fifteen fine sable furs, which he himself has bagged and would like to sell to us. Now we are up to almost three hundred furs. Far from what we had hoped, but all the same better than when we left Nelemnoye.

When we return to the jeep, we see Rayon standing in front of the administration building, looking at us in contempt along with a group of local hunters. For some reason, it does not affect me. It is as if I know deep down that Sakhabult, like the Soviet Union, is on its way to being written out of history. An organization that is so corrupt and lacking in the humility toward power that Germagen sought cannot exist forever. The collapse of Sakhabult is still awaited, but already I now sense the angel of a new revolution pass through the air.

ON THE RUN IN
THE WILDERNESS

4

I CARESS HELENE WITH MY GAZE, her fine, pale face, plump red lips, and jet-black hair that falls in wisps around her ears. Quite slowly and tenderly, I lay my arm around her throat. With my other hand, I open a button on her shirt and glimpse her white, round breasts, which peek forth from beneath her lingerie. She leans forward and whispers in my ear, "Rane, come home to me." Her words dart through me like a stream of light, and I give in. At once I feel my whole body shake.

"What's happening? Who's there?" I roar, jumping up in bed.

"Easy now, it's only me," replies Ivan, who is standing shaking me impatiently by the shoulder. He is fully dressed in winter jacket, mittens, and a big fox-fur cap, which is pulled down over his head.

"What the hell is the time?" I ask, dazed and rubbing my eyes.

"I suppose it's half past four. Get up and pack your things." Ivan goes over toward the door but stops for a moment. "We're leaving right away. The police are on the way from Zyryanka to arrest you."

It is the beginning of January. It has been a week since I returned to Siberia after ten days of vacation in St. Petersburg. There I had waved goodbye to Uffe, who had hurried home to Copenhagen to receive the many sable furs that we had bought during the month of December and that we both supposed were now on their way and

PREVIOUS: Sable hunting in the Siberian wilderness.

FACING: The author *(right)* holds a dead hare next to Ivan Danilov and the hunting dogs.

would soon reach the Danish fur auctions. As for myself, I stayed in St. Petersburg, where I was to meet my girlfriend of four years, Helene. My expectations for our reunion had grown out of proportion during our many months of separation, and in hindsight disappointment was lurking just around the corner.

And indeed our meeting was characterized from the start by a strange, oppressive deadness. Helene told me that her father had fallen sick and lay dying. She was in shock, and even though she never said it directly, her sad gaze showed that she clearly wanted me to come back to Denmark. As for myself, I was physically and mentally exhausted after the many months in Siberia and felt only emptiness in my heart. Helene had become so strangely irrelevant, obsolete to me. I was determined to go back to the Yukaghirs to drive the fur project on and to complete my fieldwork. When we parted, our relationship was in tatters. I stood at the airport and watched her disappear into the throng of busy travelers, with a sick feeling of having failed her at the worst conceivable moment. Nevertheless, I went back to northeastern Siberia with the clear expectation that the fur project was now on track.

But the situation would turn out to be quite different. When I landed in Zyryanka, I was met by Ivan, who was quite nervous. He explained to me that Shadrin had been arrested. Nobody knew why or where he was now.

In addition, all the sable furs had been confiscated. The news came as a shock.

Also, Ivan told me that there were rumors that the police in Zyryanka were awaiting an arrest warrant for "the Dane," who was to be imprisoned for illegal trade and poaching. He urged me to jump on the same plane I had arrived on, back to Yakutsk and on to Denmark.

Should I really go back? My decision was a difficult one, since rumors of my imminent arrest had also been rampant when Uffe and I were gathering furs, but had not been followed by actual problems with the forces of law and order. The police from Zyryanka had turned up only once, but since our passports and papers had been in order, they had left us in peace. I considered for a while, and then I told Ivan, in a tone that did not invite negotiation, that "it may be that the fur project is now in ruins, but I still have my fieldwork to complete."

Ivan nodded reluctantly. Next, he ordered me up on the back of the snowmobile, and with the throttle fully open, we left Zyryanka and roared away toward Nelemnoye.

For the first few days we heard nothing, and I began to think that the rumors about the arrest warrant were false as usual.

But now it was serious. Yura Spiridonov had arrived from Zyryanka on his snowmobile and brought Ivan the information that the police were on their way to Nelemnoye to arrest me. Although I should have been prepared for this, it still came as a shock as I considered the implications: What will they do once they have got me behind bars? They must have been bribed by the people at Sakhabult, who have presumably ordered my imprisonment. In the best-case scenario, I will be deported from Yakutia. In the worst case, they will kill me and pretend that it was an accident, or else they will send me to one of Yakutsk's infamous prisons, where I will either be abused and killed by the other prisoners or die of tuberculosis. All of the scenarios are gruesome. Now it is a matter of getting away, of fleeing out into the wilderness with my life intact.

When I step out into the yard, it is dark. Despite overtures to the heavens, the sun never really comes out in winter. It rummages among the icy mists for a half-hour at dawn but does not show more than a sleepy eye, and before you know it, it has completed its dozy day's work and is gone again. Among the silhouettes around me, I glimpse not just Ivan but also Yura and Slava Sinitskiy, who are sitting ready on their snowmobiles with heavily packed sleds.

"Friends in need!" I think, flinging myself up on one of the sleds. A little group of dogs gallop after the caravan with lolling tongues. They will be quite decisive for our survival in the taiga.

It is Yura who has planned our flight route, which leads toward the upper course of the Omulevka River, close to the Kolyma mountain range, about one hundred miles south of Nelemnoye. Here his father, Spiridon Spiridonov, once built a little hunting cabin, and the route to it is too long and difficult for the police with their worn-out snowmobiles to try to follow us. The plan is that Ivan and I will be left in the cabin and hunt sable for a month. After that, Yura himself will come and fetch me and take me to Spiridon and his hunting party, where I will stay until things have quieted down.

Out of Civilization

The trip to the cabin takes nearly a week. Only once, about thirty miles from Nelemnoye, do we encounter habitation. It is a wretched, neglected, remote log cabin. When we arrive, we are met by barking dogs, but nobody comes out to greet us. Yura shouts in, but the residents of the cabin only respond with a faint mumble. In the end we step in without further ado. In the light from a small window, I can make out two figures: an elderly man with a bald, spherical head, and a young man whose face is almost covered by long, disheveled hair. Both of them are wearing old, tattered clothes.

Everything about the cabin and its two inhabitants gives a dreary, sinister impression. It is as if we have arrived in a forsaken world, cut off from all cheer and energy. With his bedraggled head resting on his frightfully scrawny arms, the young man stares at us with a profoundly vacuous gaze. The old man seems completely indifferent and scarcely heeds us. He lies on the bunk, staring up at the ceiling.

"Father and son," Yura explains. "Like other hunters, they have left Nelemnoye and settled permanently in the taiga, where there is always meat to be had. But these two have been living alone for the last seven years without visiting the village."

He indicates with his hand that the two are now half crazy from silence and that I should take no notice of their odd manner. Next he looks down into the pot that is standing on the oven and exclaims triumphantly, "Muskrat! Is it okay if we eat some?" The old man just mumbles in response. Yura lays the cooked animal on a piece of wood and begins to peel the meat from the bones with his knife.

The meal is not exactly appetizing. For one thing, the muskrat really resembles a rat, with rodent teeth and a long, rough tail. For another thing, all four of us eat with our fingers, which are filthy. But I must say, the meat tastes quite good. After a stop of only an hour, we get ready to move on. As thanks for the hospitality, we leave a bottle of vodka on the table, but the residents of the cabin seem not to notice it at all. The last thin thread to civilization has now been cut. In front of us lies only the limitless and hostile terrain of the taiga.

■ ■ ■

Our little caravan of snowmobiles moves slowly forward through the silent landscape. I am sitting curled up on one of the attached sleds in an extremely uncomfortable position with my knees almost up under my chin and my back leaning against a sack of provisions. The sack was originally laid there as a back support, but now, after a long time traveling, the sled's constant bouncing up and down between the grass tussocks has turned it into an instrument of pure torture. I am totally broken on the rack, and I have bruises up and down my back.

We constantly have to stop to remove toppled tree trunks or to shovel stuck snowmobiles free from the snow. In contrast to Sinitskiy, both Ivan and Yura are fairly short of stature but robust and brawny. The do everything by muscle power—hop out into snow drifts, drag the snowmobile ski free, lift the overturned and heavily laden sled, and turn it in the direction of travel. The whole time they work with competence and admirable stamina.

At one point I think I can see a flickering gleam in the distance, as if from a bonfire, but Yura advises me to pay no attention to it.

"The forest sends hallucinations," he explains. "Sometimes it's as if it dreams like a human."

At night we pitch a tent made of thick canvas. The Yukaghir hunters formerly did not build log cabins at all but slept in tents—even in winter. And contrary to my expectations, the experience is not bad at all. Despite the cold, which is now 76 degrees below, we sit with our shirtsleeves rolled up, eating and drinking tea. In the little metal stove, the kindling crackles, and the flames quickly warm the tent up to sauna temperatures. But in the morning, when the fire has gone out, it is almost unbearably cold in the tent, and when I wake up, my eyebrows and stubble are covered in frost. Sinitskiy and I shave ourselves meticulously, as facial hair in the cold is a great nuisance. It quickly becomes moist from the breath and is transformed into a big lump of ice. As Asians, Ivan and Yura have almost no facial hair growth and can make do with pulling the hairs out with a tweezers.

Shortly before we reach the source of the Omulevka River, Yura shoots a bull moose. It weighs about thirteen hundred pounds. The moose in Siberia have adapted to the difficult living conditions and the harsh cold by becoming giants, making the moose we know from Scandinavia look like dwarfs.

"This is what you have to live on. Remember to go back and build a solid rack so that the predators can't get at it," he warns Ivan and me, while he opens the animal with quick cuts and pulls the stomach out. In extremely cold temperatures, the butchering must go at lightning speed before the dead animal freezes completely solid. We cover the meat with snow and move on.

Claws in the Wall

Spiridon's hunting cabin is in no way impressive: thirteen feet long, ten feet wide, and built from unfinished logs. Around the joints, accumulations of ice scales gleam. The Siberian cold has eaten its fill and consumed the massive beams. The floor is earthen and as hard as the permafrost itself, and the ceiling is too low to stand upright.

A feeble light filters in through the cabin's only window, a transparent plastic bag that is nailed down around a hole in the wall, and it is only just possible to glimpse the contents: two roughly crafted wooden bunks, where two people can only barely sleep, a small table, a rusty metal stove, and a kerosene lamp. A bear has been visiting and left its signature in the form of an enormous paw print on the wall but has not touched the furniture or fittings. Yura regards this as a signal from the bear to us that it is our "neighbor" and wishes to live in peace with us.

"If it had wanted conflict, it would have torn the cabin's furniture apart," he explains.

Among the Yukaghirs, the bear is regarded as a powerful shaman who functions as an intermediary between the spirit of the forest and the prey animals, just like the indigenous peoples' own shamans. Before they were persecuted and killed during Stalin's antireligion campaigns in the 1930s, shamans functioned as mediators between the spirits and humans. In fact, some hunters, including Yura, regard the bear as a physical manifestation of the "owner" of the forest (Yukaghir, *Lebie'-po'gil*), and so he is always referred to by the respectful term of kinship "Grandfather."

The bear's special, elevated status among the Yukaghirs, as among many other northern hunting peoples, probably has less to do with its size and strength than with its special, anthropomorphic qualities. Like humans, it is omnivorous, and the tracks it leaves in the form of prints and excrement are amazingly similar to our own.

There is no doubt that the bear is an intelligent animal, and its body and facial expressions are reminiscent of humans. In fact, Yura asserts that a bear will weep if it is injured. It can also sit and stand on its hind legs, just as we can, and then there is a disturbing resemblance between the construction of the body of a human and a bear when it has been skinned: abdomen, back, legs, arms—even its paws resemble our hands and feet. All of this supports the idea that the animal is a kind of human in disguise. As the British anthropologist Tim Ingold writes, "One is indeed inclined to wonder whether, if bears did not exist, men would nevertheless have conjured up in their imagination a beast of almost identical kind."[1]

Under normal circumstances, Yukaghirs refrain from hunting the bear, simply because they are afraid of its spirit, which is said to want to take revenge on the murderer. A hunter who has killed many bears is known as *metvetiatnik,* which means something like "bear-marked," and is a person who lives life dangerously. It is said that other bears are always on the lookout for him and will take any opportunity to avenge the dead member of their own species. There is a Russian hunter in Nelemnoye who is called by this nickname. Yura once went hunting with the man, and when they went back to their tent late at night, it had been visited by a bear. The strange thing was that the bear had only destroyed the Russian's things: his sleeping bag had been torn up, and his backpack lay in pieces outside the tent. But the animal had not so much as touched Yura's things, which lay exactly where he had left them. Yura's explanation for the incident was that the Russian was a *metvetiatnik* and so was hated by the bears.

Bear Paranoia

I remember all too vividly the paranoia that gripped me after I killed my first bear. It was during the expedition to the Yukaghirs in 1993. My girlfriend at the time, Ida, was with us on the trip. We had met each other a few weeks before leaving, in Café Dan Turèll in Copenhagen, where we had stood shoulder to shoulder at the bar, thoroughly squashed between well-kempt yuppies and hipsters.

I had just come home from a long field study in southern Siberia. I had not yet had a haircut or shaven and all in all looked like a real "mountain man." It must have made an impression on Ida, because after the first meeting we spent every single evening in each other's company. During the day she concentrated on her bachelor thesis in Danish literature, while my time was spent preparing for the next expedition to Siberia only a month later.

We never spoke about the forthcoming separation, probably because then it was easier to pretend to both ourselves and each other that we were not in love. But just a week before my departure, I could no longer keep my feelings to myself, and I asked, almost a little casually, whether she would like to come along on the expedition. Just as casually, she went along with the idea, and some weeks later we were on our way down the Korkodon River in northeastern Siberia in the company of a group of young researchers and a film crew from Nordisk Film.

One morning in July, Ida and I took our canoe and paddled away from the camp to enjoy each other's company in peace. Without considering it any further, I took my rifle with me, in case I should be so lucky as to bump into a moose. We sat down on a stony bank where the heat of the baking sun kept the mosquitoes away. We had bathed in the river, made love, and lay exhausted on our backs when I was woken by a deep growling sound and heavy footsteps striking the ground. When I drowsily tilted my head back, I saw a big brown bear running at full power directly toward us. Almost by reflex, I grabbed the rifle and fired off two shots in quick succession at the bear, which let out an enormous, plaintive roar and tumbled over in the high grass. I turned toward Ida, who had gone into shock and was sitting screaming hysterically.

When I again turned my gaze toward the bear, I could no longer catch sight of it. Terrified at standing alone against an injured bear, I ordered Ida to walk slowly back toward the camp to fetch help. What I did not tell her was that an injured bear will always attack a moving object, namely, Ida. A little reluctantly, she moved away along the river bank in the direction of the camp. My plan was to kill the bear in the roughly thirty yards it would have to run before it would reach her. But the bear did not show itself. The film crew did, however, as it had heard the shots and come running with the camera and all of the technical equipment at the ready. I only just managed to get my trousers on before I was caught on film.

Together we located the bear, which was trying to get up on its forelegs before falling back into the blood-soaked grass again. The big animal was hit in the chest and could not get up. With a well-placed shot to the back of the neck, I put an end to its suffering. At first I was proud of my hunting prowess, but the feeling quickly turned to fright when our two Yukaghir guides looked worriedly at me and warned me that from now on I would always have to be on guard. The bear's "brothers" would in all probability try to avenge it. For the rest of the expedition I lived like a persecuted man. I always went around with a loaded rifle, even in camp, and every time I looked out into the landscape, I thought I could glimpse the shadow of a bear sneaking around. Fortunately, nothing ever happened.

■   ■   ■

However, that is not the only time I have been struck by what I call "bear paranoia." In 1992 I was on an expedition in northern Kamchatka with my twin brother, Eske, and my friend and anthropologist colleague Morten Axel Pedersen. This is the area in Siberia that has the densest population of brown bears, living primarily on Pacific salmon that make their way up the rivers in enormous numbers to breed. In the evening, when we were lying in our tent, we constantly heard sounds that we thought came from bears. Usually, the source of the sounds was as harmless as a beetle crawling across the stretched-out canvas, or a fox that had strayed into camp.

But we had to be on guard, because who knew what it sounded like when there was a bear walking around in a tent encampment. Well, we finally found out one night. The worst thing was that we were not even armed. At first we heard heavy steps and a hollow grunting outside the tent. After that came some seconds of silence when we lay nervously looking at each other. Then I felt the canvas being pushed in close to my head. It was the bear, sniffing the tent. Its large, wet snout ran inquisitively across the fly sheet, leaving a trail of slime on the thin nylon material. The bear was so close to me that I could feel its stinking fish breath deep down in my lungs. A cold shiver ran down my spine. I looked over at Eske and Morten, who were just as terrified as I was.

Suddenly Eske whispered that he had to pee. The intense stress must have been too much for him. I saw how he was lying in the sleeping bag, squeezing his legs convulsively together to hold onto his water.

"Lie still! It's still there," whispered Morten.

But after a little while, Eske spoke up again: "I really have got to pee."

"Then pee in your sleeping bag," I hissed in annoyance.

Eske ran his eyes down over his new, specially made goose-down sleeping bag. I could see that he was thinking it would be completely destroyed. Instead he stuck his hand out, pulled over a small plastic bucket, and carefully unzipped his sleeping bag. Eske's urination could soon be heard, followed by a soft sigh of relief. But now the tent began to move. It was the bear trying to lie across the fly sheet.

The plastic bucket tumbled around in the tumult, and the contents began to slosh around in the tent, reaching halfway up to the edge of the groundsheet Eske and I had brought. Luckily, it was the extra thick model. It was worse for Morten, who had chosen the thin version. His sleeping bag was soaked in pee, clumping the down together. Morten howled in disgust. In the same instant, from inside the tent we could hear the bear tumble off at high speed through the brush. Whether it was Morten's wail that scared the bear, I do not know. But it was gone.

Completely exhausted by the terrifying experience, and wet with sweat and urine, we sat back, staring blankly at each other. None of us had been so close to death before. We said nothing, but we were all thinking the same thing: "We will never go to bed again without having a loaded gun in the tent."

Later, Eske and a local Russian hunter located the bear and shot it. Once a bear has gone into a camp, it will in all probability return.

The Hunting Ritual

Sometimes the Yukaghirs also feel obliged to kill a bear. This happens if the bear repeatedly gets into their depots, or if there are no other animals to hunt and so people are starving. In such situations, they typically track down the bear's winter lair, which can be recognized by a rising faint cloud of sweat and the shield of piled-up ice formations it creates on top of the lair. There may also be other signs:

broken and bitten-off bushes, old bear tracks, and feces. The hunters find their way to the entrance to the lair, of which there may sometimes be several, and fill it with long logs. That stops the bear from escaping. After that, they dig a small hole from above down into the lair, stick a rifle down into it, and shoot wildly to all sides.

The problem is that one never knows how many bears there are in a single lair, or whether they have all been killed. A bear can tolerate a large loss of blood. Not even a clean shot through the heart necessarily brings the animal down. The only way to find out whether all of the bears are dead is to send a hunter into the lair. As a rule, this task falls to the youngest in the hunting group, who is given the opportunity to show his courage. He ties a rope around his waist so that he can be dragged out quickly if necessary, and then crawls down into the lair. If he sees a pair of luminous eyes, he has to get out quickly before the living or injured bear tears his head off. If, on the other hand, there is nothing to see in the dark, it means that the bears are dead, and the hunters then begin the job of digging them out of the lair.

Even in death, the bear is a frightful sight, and there is a long Yukaghir ritual associated with the killing, which has the clear objective of presenting the whole misdeed as a tragic accident that the hunters themselves are not responsible for.

They will take turns bowing to the dead bear, saying, "Grandfather, it was not me who killed you, but a Russian." After that, they cover the bear's eyes with a scarf or poke them out with a knife while they cry like ravens. That will make the bear think that it is a bird that is blinding it.[2]

While they are skinning it, they will say, "Grandfather, you must feel warm, now I'll take your coat off you."

After removing all of the meat, they place the bones, picked clean and completely white, up on a scaffold. This ritual was how Yukaghirs used to bury their deceased relatives, before they became Christian. The skull is turned toward the west and the setting sun, which is said to be the direction to the realm of the dead, or Land of Shadows (Yukaghir, *Ayibii-lebie*), as the Yukaghirs call it. As a last safety precaution, the hunters tie the jaws of the skull together with willow twigs, so that the animal's spirit cannot attack them.

5

ONLY A DAY AFTER OUR ARRIVAL at the hunting cabin in the mountains near the source of the Omulevka River, Yura and Sinitskiy head back to Nelemnoye. Our parting is brief and unsentimental. Everyone knows that Ivan and I will now have to look after ourselves in the taiga and that it will undoubtedly be a challenge, but no one mentions it. This is just the way things have developed, and from here on, we must focus on practicalities. We watch the two disappear between the trees, and soon we can no longer hear the noise of the engine. Then we are on our own, with no snowmobile but in the company of five dogs. Originally, the plan was to bring only two dogs: Bim, Spiridon's experienced old elkhound, and Jack, a young dog to be trained in hunting. But when we left Nelemnoye, three stray dogs followed our sled trail.

Bim is an old, balding white-fur with dull eyes. The muscle tissue is still visible underneath his fur, but it is clearly weak and lacking the vigor of youth. In his day, Bim was Spiridon's best elkhound. Apart from an excellent sense of smell and an almost indomitable eagerness, he also displayed remarkable intelligence. At one point, he single-handedly chased a moose into camp, where Spiridon shot it. But now Bim is old and tired. He spends most of his days curled up in the snow in front of the cabin, covering his nose with his spiral tail. Jack is just the opposite. He has a thick, black coat and a dazzling white collar. His eyes gleam with youth and energy. He is never still but constantly explores the woods around the cabin.

We have not brought much in the way of provisions: a sack of

Ivan Danilov shoots at a sable that has been trapped in a tree.

flour, a sack of macaroni, a bottle of vodka, cigarettes, some candy, sugar, and tea. That is all. But we have two guns: a small-bore rifle for small game and a magnum-caliber Mauser for big game. Both guns are old and worn. The stock of the heavy-caliber rifle has a gaping crack that has been filled with resin, and the barrel of the small-bore rifle has been severely shortened and patched with pewter. Moreover, ammunition is sparse: one hundred cartridges for the small-bore rifle, and only ten for the large-caliber one. Ivan may be familiar with hunting just like any other indigenous male in the area, but he is not an experienced hunter like Yura or Spiridon. For most of his adult life, he has made his living as an electrician in Nelemnoye. And he does not know the area. Our stay in the wilderness will prove a challenge for both him and me.

■   ■   ■

I myself started hunting at an early age, but not until the end of my prolonged stay in the Siberian taiga would I dare call myself an experienced hunter. When I was a boy, my twin brother, Eske, and I hunted small animals such as squirrels and birds, first with bows and arrows and later with an air gun. Later on, once we had our hunting licenses, we started hunting deer with rifles. This all took place around our Swedish homestead. Our elderly father was no hunter, so we had to teach ourselves how to shoot and skin game. But the old man did manage to give us one very important thing, something I have made great use of during all my travels in Siberia: dogged perseverance.

During our childhood, he threw us into the sea by the house countless times—in winter, mind you, when everything was covered in ice—and during the summer vacation, he made us chop firewood for hours on end, seven days a week. When we protested, he gave us a rap on the back of the head. It was not that the old man was mean. He undoubtedly cared for us a great deal. But he knew no way of bringing up children other than relentless strictness. He had been raised the same way as a child. He just wanted to turn us into men with the willpower to endure tough physical trials.

First Sable Hunt

On the first day after we have been left to ourselves, Ivan and I set out to explore the area. What kind of game might be living here? Each of us swings a rifle over his shoulder, and we set out down the slope in front of the cabin. A croaking raven appears in the sky. It comes closer, grows, moves away, and shrinks, showing by its flight the depth of the landscape surrounding us. It is flat and monotonous. Matchstick-thin conifer trees dot the landscape as far as the eye can see, interrupted to the east only by the ragged profiles of the mountains of the Kolyma Upland and to the south by the Omulevka River winding its way in and out between brinks of fallen trees and logs. The snow blanket is still rather thin, making it easy for the dogs to keep up.

Jack and Bim are running free while the other three dogs are pulling our sled.

The shape of the Yukaghir dogsled, the method of harnessing the dogs, and their number differ from those of the well-known dog-driving cultures of the American Arctic. The Yukaghir sled has three or four pairs of stanchions and a circular forepart. The dogs are attached to a long strap in pairs in tandem, but a full team rarely consists of more than three or four dogs. When the load is heavy, the driver is forced to don the harness himself and pull the sled together

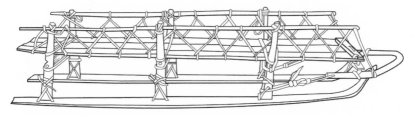

Yukaghir dogsled and harness. Drawings by Sara Heil Jensen.

with the dogs. Otherwise, he walks in front of the team, breaking the trail with his skis, and calling back to the team to urge it to follow. The harness consists of a breast piece and two or three bands across the back. The course is directed by the voice of the driver, who uses special call-words: "Hey, hey!" for "Forward!" and "Ho, ho!" for "Stop!" These are understood and obeyed by the lead dog, which is specially trained for that purpose.

In our case, however, there is no lead dog, and our three dogs have difficulties understanding the meaning of our calls. They pull in different directions, causing the sled to tip and the harness to get tangled up. After continuous shouting and beating, the dogs do better, pulling the sled in the same direction and with such energy that foam flows from their mouths. Downhill their high vigor is quite problematic, however, since the sled is liable to hit them on their hind legs and overturn. Thus, Ivan and I have to exert the utmost care to swing the sled first to the right and then to the left, and to support it by hanging down from one side or by standing on one of the runners. Luckily, our sled is empty, making it much easier to control than a heavily loaded one.

We have been walking with the dogs for about an hour when Jack turns up his nose, anxiously staring at something in the landscape. A moment later, he is gone, but then we hear barking. We tether the sled and the dogs and run toward the place to find Jack furiously circling a tree. At the top, a small black animal is darting in and out between the branches. We can only just make out its bushy tail and small, pointy ears, but its loud and jittery nature is not to be mistaken: this is a sable—Siberia's soft gold! I take the ax and start felling the surrounding trees, so the sable has no escape route. Ivan prepares the small-bore rifle and takes aim.

"Rane, you catch the sable when it falls, otherwise the dogs will tear it apart," he says.

The first three shots miss. The rifle is old, from the 1940s, and does not shoot accurately. Besides, the sable is constantly moving. But then the right moment arrives: the sable sits still, arching its tensed back while it watches its pursuers. This is probably the first time it has seen humans. Ivan shoots, the sable falls, and I catch it in the air. Fantastic.

We have collected our first sable—and such quality! Its fur is dark, almost black, with an occasional silver hair. Its chest is orange and shimmers in the light. Ivan gingerly runs his index finger up along the hairs on its back.

"Feel the fur. The hairs are so fine you almost can't feel them. The Barguzin type," he says, smiling. "There is no better quality."

The sable is put in the backpack, and Jack gets a candy for a job well done. But today's hunting adventure is not over. Jack bays a full three more times, and each time he has tracked down another sable. The quality of the fur is not as high as that of the first one, though. They are all of the *Kolymskiy Kryazh* type, with cream-colored or light brown fur. But still, four sables on our first day. Not a bad result.

On our way back to the cabin, we pass by the meat from the moose Yura shot. We consider building a rack for it, but darkness has already fallen, so we decide to wait and instead take a decent chunk of meat with us in our backpack. Once we have lit the stove fire and put water on to boil, Ivan takes the black sable out of the backpack and lays it on the bed. He strokes its back repeatedly. Then he pours a glass of vodka and tips it down the animal's throat, after which he smears a little fat on its teeth.

"What on earth are you doing?" I ask with a laugh. "Are you pouring our good spirits on a dead animal?"

Ivan is in no mood for joking and answers solemnly: "The sable must know it is our guest. Then it will tell its kinfolk they can come to us without fear."

What Ivan does next makes me choke on my tea. He takes the black sable and flings it into the fire.

"What the hell are you doing? Have you gone raving mad?" I yell.

"That's the rule," Ivan answers firmly. "The first sable must be burned."

"Why the hell should that be? The black one is our best sable," I wail, on the verge of tears.

"I don't know why, but that's the way it is," Ivan answers.

"You and your witchcraft," I snarl, throwing myself despondently on the bed. I have not yet surrendered to the hunter's view of the taiga as a place full of spirits that are just as alive as anything that breathes and that must constantly be reckoned with in our daily lives.

Ivan may be right after all, because the following weeks go like a breeze. Everywhere, sable tracks embroider the landscape, and nearly every hour we hear Jack barking, and we catch something every time. Sables are practically pouring in. Four to six a day is not unusual. We are blessed with almost divine hunting luck that seems as if it will never end.

Actually, the sable's migration routes are highly changeable and completely unpredictable, so a hunter can never know with certainty whether he will return with his pack full of sables or with only a few.

Ivan explains it in his own way. He says the forest spirits love to get drunk and play cards. They constantly play each other, with the sable and the other fur animals as their stakes. So the animals must pass from one owner to the next at the end of each game. He even tells me of hunters who try to bribe the spirits with booze. When the hunting season begins, they go out into their game preserves and leave bottles of vodka as presents for the local spirits, hoping to be rewarded in sable.

Skinning the dead sables is a time-consuming and meticulous task in the beginning. It is important not to pierce the delicate pelt. But with time and experience, we become extraordinarily fast. At my best, I can skin a sable in less than seven minutes. First, you make an incision at the animal's mouth, then at its front and hind paws, and next you carefully pull the pelt down over the animal's head. Each piece of loosened pelt is cleaned with the dull side of the knife blade. The knife is the hunter's most indispensable tool. It must be long, sharp, and heavy, as it serves many different purposes. With the sharp edge, one carves up the game or cuts wood shavings to light a fire with. The wider back edge of the blade is used to crush bones to get to the marrow, while the lowest, duller part of the edge is used to clean sable furs.

Once the pelt has been removed from the body, it is stretched out with the furry side inward on a circular stretcher made from a piece of thick steel wire, so that it stays smooth and stretched. Then the pelt is hung from the ceiling to dry. It must not get too dry, mind you, so the following day the pelt is taken off the stretcher and laid with the rest of the furs under the bed, where it stays ice-cold even if the fire in the stove is lit. Sable meat has a foul carnivorous stench and is normally eaten by neither humans nor dogs. Instead, the carcasses are laid across the branches of trees, since throwing them on the ground would be an insult to the animals.

A Strange Experience

One day, when I am out hunting on my own, I experience something strange. The dogs are out with Ivan, and I am not actually expecting to come upon any game. Having walked around for a few hours, I reach a valley where the cracked trunks of the towering larch trees reach up toward the sky. There is something tormented and ravished about them. In some places, they are sooty, as if after a forest fire, and in other places, they are red. The drooping branches are exposed and naked, as the Siberian larch sheds its needles in the winter. In the afternoon sun, the massive trunks with their drooping, needleless branches look like fiery red tents. I stroke the rough, scarred bark with my hand and stare up into the scattered branches high above me. Considering that the larches in these parts grow extremely slowly, these giants, at a height of around 150 feet, must be thousands of years old. They have been here since before the Russians and the Sakha arrived, possibly even before the old hunting peoples.

You might wonder how trees can even grow in this cold area with winter temperatures far lower than those in places like Greenland, which is practically devoid of trees. This is due to the fact that they go into a sort of hibernation mode in winter. The temperatures in this period are thus less crucial to their survival. What is crucial is the climate during the growing season. The short but very warm Siberian summer makes it possible for the trees to sustain themselves.[1]

The larch dominates Siberia's northeastern taiga. Birch and poplar are also found, and many different species of willow grow along the riverbanks. But without the larch, this otherwise dead, cold world would be uninhabitable for humans. The strength of the tree is reflected in its heating value. While poplar, birch, and willow burn like they grow—very fast—and explode like firecrackers, larch wood burns evenly for a long time, due to its slow growth and frost-hardened toughness. The larch can also be used for orientation: the side of the trunk that has dark, wasted bark and small, stunted branches always indicates north.

I decide to take a break to enjoy the beautiful weather. The temperature is quite pleasant for a change. It is only about 20 degrees below, which is unusual. At night, temperatures drop below minus 75 degrees, and in the daytime, they rarely climb above minus 60. But today, the sun is caressing my face. Using my dagger, I cut star shapes out of larch wood chips, light a fire, and boil a kettle of water for tea. As I am sitting there, far away from everything and everyone, the company of the flames is a delight. I talk to the fire with my eyes, and it responds by crackling and sparking. What happens is one of those things people rarely experience together, namely, both parties simultaneously speaking and listening to each other. I understand why the Siberian hunters consider the bonfire an organism with a soul.[2] Like them, I throw an offering into the fire—one of my cigarettes.

I am sitting in silence, admiring the fire's beautiful color play, when I suddenly notice a sable watching me curiously from a branch in a dead larch tree just a couple of yards away. Just like me, it must have been sitting there warming itself in the sun. Ivan has our smallbore rifle, while I am lugging the carbine around. If the bullet hits anything but the sable's head, it will split the fur and make it worthless. I lie down in the snow and take aim at the animal's conical head. The concentration makes me feel as if my eye is being pulled out through the rifle's sight and attached to the little round snout between the animal's ears. With a soft delay, I pull the trigger. A magnificent shot. The sable falls from the tree and lies motionless in the snow. Its body and tail are relatively short, which means it is a female.

As I lift the animal, I see a red drop of blood on top of its head. My shot has only just grazed it and left a tiny scratch. The sable's heart is still beating, and after a brief moment, it regains consciousness. I expect it to start hissing and trying to bite me, as usually happens, so I tighten my grip around its chest, in order to squeeze the life out of it. But the sable reacts quite differently. As soon as my hand closes around it, it stiffens with fear. Beneath my mitten, I can feel it heaving and trembling. It gazes up at me with big, coral-colored eyes.

Confused, I loosen my grip on the animal. Then I decide to let it go. I put it down in the snow, and it disappears into the woods in two long jumps.

"What the hell happened to me?" I mutter to myself on my way back to the fire. "Why did I let that animal get away?" Compared to our total catch of thirty furs, the loss of one single sable is quite insignificant, but I am confused by my own action.

To this day, I have no unequivocal explanation for this. Perhaps I was overcome by a momentary feeling of guilt for having killed so many of the animal's kin. Perhaps it was an awkward attempt to defy the taiga's relentless law of the stronger party having the advantage and unscrupulously taking advantage of it. I do not know. But the fact is I do not mention it to Ivan, as I am afraid he will think I have been afflicted with wilderness delirium.

You Share Your Catch

There are sable pelts hanging up to dry all over our small cabin, giving off a dense rotten stench. But Ivan and I do not care. We barely take the time to chop firewood, rest, or eat. Even before sunrise, we are out of our sleeping bags and hunting. We must reap while the snow blanket is still thin and Jack can run around freely. Without Jack, we would never have caught so many sables. The dog has proven to be a natural at sable hunting. Bim, on the other hand, is only interested in moose and does not even react to a sable standing right under his nose. This is mainly because Bim is Spiridon's dog. His specialty is moose, not sable.

"Why is Spiridon not interested in sable when it's teeming with them at Omulevka?" I ask.

Ivan ponders this for a moment, then answers, "Whatever you and Uffe might think, the Yukaghirs aren't really interested in sable. It's moose they go after. You can see for yourself how they share everything, whether it's meat, cigarettes, or gasoline. If a Yukaghir has something of use, one family member after the other will show up demanding his or her share. So it's not really attractive for a Yukaghir hunter to hunt sable. He may be able to buy valuable stuff with the money he gets for his furs, but he won't get to keep it anyway—his family will make sure of that. So moose is much better. The meat is also shared, but now at least the hunter is shown respect. In Nelemnoye, you'll see how the old people make a chattering noise with their teeth when they meet Spiridon, and they say, 'When your luck is good, we all have food.' It's a tribute to Spiridon, because with his meat, he feeds everybody else."

I am deeply fascinated by what Ivan tells me about the Yukaghirs' selfless distribution of nature's resources, and I ask more questions about the topic: "How about under Communism—did the state farm force Spiridon to hunt sable?"

Ivan shakes his head. "You must understand that the Yukaghirs had an entirely different moral code from the Soviets'. If a hunter came home with lots of sable furs, people would ridicule him: 'What kind of filthy furs have you got there? Those can't be sable; look how ugly and lousy they are . . . ' The hunter was humiliated in this way to stop his success going to his head. Spiridon knew this was how it was. That is why he always told the state farm there were not many sables to be had at Omulevka. Then they left him in peace, and he could spend all his time hunting moose.

"The other Yukaghirs feel the same way. When I settled in Ne-lemnoye at the start of the 1970s, I had a very hard time understanding why the Yukaghir hunters never fulfilled the state farm's plan for sable, while the Russian and Sakha hunters in Verkhne Kolymsk and Aralakh always did, sometimes by several hundred percent, despite the fact that there are far more sables in the Yukaghirs' territory. Now I have learned that the Yukaghirs do not strive for personal wealth and so are not particularly interested in hunting sable."

■ ■ ■

Among the Soviet anthropologists, the idea prevailed that present-day Yukaghir society has vestiges, or "survivals," of the original matriarchy, in which the woman was the head of the family and wielded political power. This is why, they claim, women among the Yukaghirs generally enjoy a great respect and esteem and are allowed to hunt on equal terms with the men.[3] It is quite possible that the assertion of an original matriarchy was mostly politically driven by the Soviet power's attempt to discover the cradle of Communism. But the fact remains that among the Yukaghirs there prevails a fundamental financial and social equality among everyone, women and men.

Ivan's explanation raises a swarm of thoughts in my head. If the Yukaghirs' way of distributing resources makes them uninterested in hunting sable, would the Danish–Yukaghir Fur Project be doomed right from the outset? The project ultimately rested on the idea that everybody is driven by the desire for personal wealth. But if the Yukaghirs deliberately prevent inequality by sharing everything and therefore do not have an immediate incentive to save money and other goods, it is hard to see how the fur project would ever work. For what would be the hunter's motivation to hunt sable in large quantities if his profit from selling the furs would be shared with the rest of the village anyway?

Or even worse: If the fur project had created the necessary motivation, what consequences would it have had for the people's traditional way of distributing resources? Would the project have crushed the Yukaghirs' principle of equality instead of contributing to their survival? As I gain a greater insight into the hunters' way of life, I begin to doubt the very idea behind the fur project. Its potential for improving the Yukaghirs' lives no longer seems so obvious.

Greedy Foxes

"We're turning into foxes," Ivan mutters to me one morning as we lie in our sleeping bags, dreading the thought of stepping out into the cold to light the stove.

"How do you mean?" I ask.

"Smell the stench!" he replies. "And look at all these furs, hanging around like the greedy fox's trophies. We're living like filthy predators, filthy foxes. Wolverines, wolves, and foxes all have an irresistible greed and bloodlust. If given the chance, they will kill any form of prey they encounter. They are sinful (Russian, *gryaznyy*) creatures. We say that they are 'children of the devil' (Russian, *chërtovyye deti*). Similarly, a human person who kills recklessly is called a 'son of the devil' (Russian, *chërtovyy syn*). Sooner or later, he will pay for his sins. Let's have a break for a few days to find ourselves again."

I say nothing but gradually ease myself out of the bunk and light the stove. Soon we are sitting sipping tea.

Yet our ease does not last long. We hear Jack barking a hundred yards away. Ivan picks up his gun, and we jog out to start another day of shooting all round us.

Ivan fires a shot at the sable, which is clinging on, partly hidden by the trunk of the tree it has climbed. The shot misses, and the sable scampers along a branch and leaps into the next tree, and the next. Ivan fires again. The sable takes another leap but falls to the ground and begins to run away, with Jack in hot pursuit.

Ivan and I run stumbling through the snow after Jack and the sable.

Jack finally trees the animal again. Ivan steadies himself on one knee, shoots, and knocks the sable out of the tree. I catch it in the air and put it in the bag before Jack can seize it.

It is only later, when we are back at the cabin, that I notice that I have lost all but four cartridges for our high-power rifle.

"Better go carefully from now on," says Ivan, staring solemnly at the depleted ammunition. I sense the beginning of a new situation in which the dark side of our excessive hunting luck is about to reveal its deadly face.

6

STARVATION AND DESPERATION

A MONTH AND A HALF has passed since we arrived at the hunting cabin. The sack of sable furs is bulging, but the chunk of meat has long since been eaten. Several times, we have gone to get meat from the moose Yura shot, but without building an actual rack for the meat. We decide to make another excursion to the moose meat and bring more back to the cabin. When we reach the place, it stinks like an old urinal. A wolverine has been there and finished off the meat.

"Damned thief!" Ivan snaps and spits in the snow. "Didn't leave us so much as a bone splinter."

Like the sable, the wolverine is a member of the Mustelidae family, but it looks more than anything like a small bear, apart from its long, bushy tail. It is known as the greediest of all the predators in the taiga, feeding mainly on prey killed by others. To guard against other scavengers, it pees on the carcass, making it completely inedible to all others. Although the wolverine weighs only thirty to forty-five pounds, it does not shy away from carrying off large chunks of meat several times its own weight. That is why you can sometimes find entire moose heads high up in trees, where the wolverine has taken them.

Trappers hate the wolverine, because it steals from their traps and meat caches. A hunter who caught a wolverine that had given him trouble for a while went so far as to shoot it in the knees and elbows and to leave it for the dogs to bite to death. It sounds brutal, but that is life in the taiga for animals and humans alike. In this place,

Ivan Danilov is bedridden from frostbite and starvation.

you live by killing and avoiding getting killed. There is no room for feeling sorry for your enemy or your prey. This does not mean, however, that the wolverine is seen to be fundamentally evil by nature. In fact, a sort of myth flourishes among the trappers of the region, in which it is told that the wolverine did not become the hunter's worst enemy until the hunter himself had betrayed it.

As the tale goes, the wolverine and the hunter were originally the best of friends—even better than the hunter and his dog in our time. This is because at the dawn of time there was a hunter who took a wolverine cub in and raised it as his hunting dog. Never before nor since has anyone seen such an excellent hunting dog. The hunter did not have to accompany it on the hunt at all. The wolverine used to kill the prey by itself and bring it back to the hunter. The wolverine made the hunter the richest man in the region. But his riches made him greedy—he wanted even more money. When a trader came passing through, wanting to buy the fantastic wolverine, the hunter sold his friend. The wolverine was taken far away and put on show in a circus. But one day, it ran away and set out on the long journey back to the hunter. When the hunter saw the wolverine, he said, "Hello, my friend. How nice to see you back, as I'm out of money. Now you must hunt for me and make me rich." But the wolverine wanted revenge. It jumped on the hunter and bit him across the throat. That was the end of the friendship between hunter and wolverine. Ever since, the wolverine has been stealing from the hunter to get back everything it once gave him.

The wolverine's tufted and unsightly fur did not become attractive as a trading commodity until sometime in the 1960s. Since the animal's long, bristly hairs do not freeze, even under the most extreme temperatures, wolverine fur is used in Russian space science for the cosmonauts' masks, and good money is generally paid for the fur. Many trappers, including myself, also wear caps made from wolverine fur. However, it is most suitable for travel by snowmobile or dogsled. On foot or skis, wolverine fur is simply too warm and heavy to wear on one's head.

Wolverine fur is also excellent as a back compress. For many years, I regularly suffered from severe back pains, until a fellow anthropologist brought me a piece of wolverine fur from northern Mongolia. When I put it on my back, my pain subsides after a few hours.

Unfortunately, the wolverine is hard to catch. It is an incredibly cunning animal, which is not easily lured into a trap. Even if that happens, the animal often escapes by twisting the trap into pieces with its powerful jaws.

■　■　■

Personally, I have managed to bag a wolverine only once, and that was a matter of luck. It was in 1992, when I was on a six-month field trip in the northern Altai Mountains, close to the Mongolian border.[1] I was out hunting birds when I saw my dog running around down by the river, barking like mad. It turned out that the dog had encountered a wolverine. From a distance, I could just make out its wide, very flat skull, with the whitish spot between its eyes and its small, oval ears. The wolverine was arching its back, with its eyes aflame and its mouth menacingly open, showing its fangs. The dog had the good sense not to engage in close combat. The front paw of a full-grown wolverine is enough to rip open the stomach of a dog, so it would not stand a chance in a fight.

I managed to get within shooting range of the wild animal, and I killed it. Everything was fine and dandy until I started skinning it. In my ignorance of the wolverine's anatomy, I inadvertently pierced its tail gland, and a dirty yellow secretion with a sickening stench sprayed out over my hands and legs. Ugh! Disgusting! For the rest of the week, I was giving off this horrible, acrid smell that made all the animals of the forest trek around me at a wide radius.

Turn of Fortune

Without our cache of moose meat, we are suddenly left with no food, and snow has started falling heavily, so the dogs sink in and are unable to accompany us on the hunt. The sable tracks are farther and farther apart, and we catch almost nothing. For hours on end, we struggle through the snow-clad wilderness without catching so much as a glimpse of an animal. Every once in a while we come across old moose tracks and hardened excrement. But all the tracks are cold and more or less decayed. Although we set snares for hares and grouse and even manage to catch a few, our stomachs are never satisfied.

The deep snow has forced us to use leghold traps. A leghold trap is a kind of restraining trap. Its metal jaws close around the sable's front leg and restrain the animal without killing it. The cold, the hunger, and the stress of being restrained kill the animal. Relative to the work that goes into setting the traps, hunting with leghold traps is scarcely profitable.

First, the hunter must find a trail, that is, a place where the sable comes frequently. Then, with his ski, he shovels up a pile of snow next to the track. Once the pile is the right size—around three feet high—he digs a hollow in the pile and places a piece of bait at the inner end of it. Then he makes a small depression in front of the bait, lays some sticks lengthwise, and places the open trap on top of it all. This is to prevent the spring mechanism from freezing to ensure that the trap will snap. For the same reason, the hunter also places a piece of thin paper over the trap, and lastly he covers everything in loose snow so that all looks natural. Finally, the hunter typically says a sort of magical incantation over the trap.

Each hunter has his own words, and these are Ivan's: "I stand here, God's servant, Ivan. I make the sign of the Cross and walk in prayer for blessing. I set the trap for the black sable. May it bring me luck!" But it is all to no avail. Our luck is almost entirely gone. Even though we set almost fifty traps, we catch only four sables.

The problem is that success in trap hunting requires a lot of experience, because it is usually curiosity rather than hunger that drives the sable to the bait. For this very reason, Tayson Arkadiy, a hunter from Verkhne Kolymsk, does not use meat as bait but old cigarette packages and other pieces of junk, which he soaks in gasoline. The smell and the bright colors pique the sable's curiosity and drive it into the trap. Only the most skillful sable hunters have developed that kind of sophisticated trick. To inexperienced hunters like Ivan and myself, it is pure luck if a sable falls into our trap.

Getting Serious

It is hard for an outsider to imagine how much energy a hunter in the taiga needs on a daily basis. I once read that a lumberjack

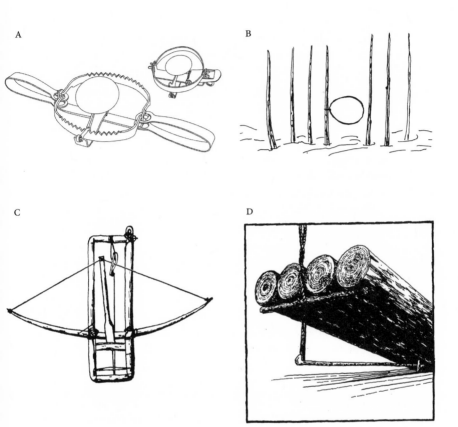

Traps. (a) Metal leghold trap for wolf and sable. (b) Steel-wire snare for hare.
(c) Wooden bow trap for ermine. (d) Timber deadfall trap for wolverine.
Drawings by Jens Kirkeby.

metabolizes more energy than any other occupation: 5,500 calories a day. However, I think the trapper's metabolism outdoes that. In a wilderness with neither roads nor paths, where you have to wade ten to fifteen miles a day through snow in conditions where the temperature does not get above 60 degrees below zero, you consume vast amounts of energy.

This means that the daily ration of meat a hunter needs to be able to work is around nine pounds, not even including fat, which is invariably consumed in large quantities. It is simply a matter of consuming the largest possible amount of calories. And despite these huge amounts of meat and fat, constant weight loss cannot be avoided when working as a trapper in the taiga.

At this point, food has been scarce for weeks, and we have not eaten anything at all for an entire week. Hunger has left visible marks on our bodies. I put my hand up under my shirt and feel my stomach. This past week, it has burned very badly in there. The piercing discomfort has gone by now, but even so my entire body is now experiencing the highest degree of pain. My arms and legs ache, and I can barely carry them. Even the act of lighting a fire in the stove is immensely tiring.

We are moving into the final phase of starvation. If we do not get something to eat soon, we will be too weak to go hunting. And then we will be seriously doomed. We feed the dogs rotten carcasses from the skinned sables. Initially, they are not keen to touch the foul-smelling predator meat, but hunger is more powerful than anything else, and soon they start fighting madly for the cadavers. Jack bites one of the stray dogs to death, and the others ravenously jump on their peer and devour him. As the days pass, I knock the other dogs on the head with my ax and feed their meat to Jack and Bim. Only the useful dogs are allowed to live.

As if that were not enough, Ivan has contracted frostbite in his right foot. The foot is swollen, the skin is cracked, oozing a foul liquid, and he is unable to move his toes. We see no sign of black spots, meaning it is only second-degree frostbite, so the foot does not need to be amputated, but it is painful enough to stop him walking around, and he is bedridden in the cabin.

For my own part, I was also afflicted with an almost unbearable pain when my right molar suddenly cracked crosswise. Why it happened I do not know. Perhaps the piping hot tea we had been drinking in large quantities, combined with the extreme cold, made the tooth crack. At any rate, I have noticed that practically every hunter has lost some or all of his teeth.

I soon developed a nasty gumboil. At first, I was hoping the inflammation would subside on its own. But it did not. Eventually, it became so painful that I took my jackknife and pulled out the pliers. Just touching the tooth sparked a dart of pain that almost made me pass out. Then I mustered my courage, grabbed the tooth with the pliers, and tore it out. The pain pierced my skull with such a lash that I saw huge peacock eyes glide past me. To stop the blood gushing out, I filled my mouth repeatedly with snow. The roots of the tooth must have stayed behind, for they sprang out of my swollen gums one by one during the days that followed, and I had to take the pliers again to pull them out.

Shatun

We are woken one night by the dogs barking like crazy. We open the cabin door and look out, but the darkness is too dense for us to see anything. The next morning, only a few hundred yards from the cabin, I discover some tracks in the snow. They are as wide as shovel blades, and only one animal could have left such tracks. I race back to Ivan, who stutters in a terrified voice, "Shatun!" This is the Russian word for a bear that prowls around in winter, desperately looking for food.

For the bear to be able to hibernate, it must have built up a decent store of fat underneath its fur. It must have something to consume during up to eight months of hibernation. But if, for one reason or another, it does not succeed, because of old age or injury, it cannot remain in hibernation but must go out hunting. These bears are called *shatun* bears. They are crazy from hunger and will attack anything, including humans. What is worse, the body's condensed perspiration and the hard frost turn the bear's fur into a thick ice shell, serving as a kind of bulletproof armor. So you cannot be sure of killing a *shatun* bear unless you shoot it in the armpits or through the mouth, which is hard if it comes charging right at you.

Should you decide to hunt a *shatun*, it is essential to have your back covered, as the bear can come back in a circle, pursuing you in your own tracks, which completely reverses the situation. The bear is now on your back. This happened to a hunter from Nelemnoye. The attacking bear sneaked up on him, scalped him, and tore his eye out. It was only because his son managed to get a lethal shot at the bear that the hunter survived.

We sit in silence, gazing into space. Neither of us knows how to handle the situation. Not only has our prey vanished from the face of the earth, we risk becoming prey ourselves when we go out hunting.

"If it's the bear that left his mark in the wall, it's a whopper," Ivan observes despondently. "And if so, it will take several shots to kill it."

He looks at the empty tin can containing the remainder of our ammunition. There are only four of the large cartridges left, thanks to our breakneck sable hunt.

I fling my metal mug at the wall. The hopeless situation has made the anger blaze up in me: "Where the hell has Yura gone? He said a month, then he and the others would come and get us, but it's been almost two months!"

Ivan says nothing but rolls over on the bed and pulls his sleeping bag up over his head. He is too weak to carry on the conversation and dozes off, while I lean back on the bed, close my eyes, and become more and more drowsy. I feel my head emptying in a quiet slumber until at last it is completely devoid of thoughts.

An Omen

That night, eerie visions float before my eyes. I am wandering through a dark coniferous forest, much like the one around us, and arrive at a small, wretched cabin that looks roughly like our own. There is a woman standing in there, whom I can only just make out in the light from the window. Her long black hair falls like wet drapery down over her naked body. She stands completely motionless, pointing at the bunk, where a child is lying swaddled in animal hide. A thin streak of blood seeps from one of the child's eyes.

Horrified, I turn my face toward the woman, who takes my hand smilingly and places it on her breast. I feel fatty milk streaming out between my fingers. She presses me tightly against her, greedily pressing her body against mine, smiling all the while. Warmth radiates from her body, and I feel her breath blowing right in my face. Desire courses through me in the form of ravenous hunger. I must penetrate her breast with my mouth, and I topple her over onto the floor, throw myself on top of her, and eagerly suck in the warm, creamy milk.

When I get up, she lies lifeless on the floor. Her eyes stare at me, dry and protruding like horns, and not a muscle moves in her face. She is dead. The hunger is still gnawing at my chest, and I start ripping the bloody meat off her bones, eating it more and more greedily. I swallow large chunks without chewing. Completely gorged, I stand up and wipe the blood off my mouth with my shirtsleeve. I look down at the half-eaten human cadaver, and now the shame wells up in me, glowing and brutal. I feel like a creep, gripped by devastation. I hate my entire shrunken body, and I am disgusted to feel it around me.

■   ■   ■

An ominous jolt shoots through my nerves, making me jump up off the bunk. It is pitch-black and bitingly cold. I lie back in my sleeping bag with a nauseating taste in my mouth, thinking, "What the hell does that dream mean? Is it my mad hunger trying to force me to eat my fellow humans?" Among the Yukaghirs, I have heard terrifying stories of how in earlier times starvation drove people to kill their old and young to eat them.[2]

I lie still while it gets brighter and brighter outside the window. I can now partially make out Ivan, who is completely motionless. I actually start wondering if he is dead. But then I hear his soft breathing. Only a little bit of his black hair is jutting out from under his sleeping bag. He looks tremendously small lying there. When all the fat has been burned off, leaving only muscle and bones, the volume of the body shrinks, and you start looking like nothing more than a bony old man.

"He wouldn't make much of a meal," I think, laughing hoarsely to myself.

People who find themselves face-to-face with death often exhibit a sort of ironic contempt for the situation, which is really just a result of the fear of facing it. I do not want to go out that way. I make a firm decision, get out of my sleeping bag, and get dressed. I quickly jot down a few lines, a farewell letter to my twin brother, Eske.

The letter says that whether or not we ever see each other again, the two of us are really all there has ever been.

"Our dad impressed on us from an early age that the desire for knowledge is the most important thing. You sought it through biology, and I through anthropology. And we both sought it in the Siberian wilds. But the actual goal of our strenuous journeys has not been science but just each other. For your sake, I wanted to research the Yukaghirs; for my sake, you had to find the mammoth's DNA. Only people who do not understand what it means to be identical twins would call it mutual competition."

I fold the letter and put it in my inside pocket, together with my passport. That should be enough to identify my rigid-frozen corpse, if it comes to that. In my letter, I ask that my body, should it be found, be carefully brought back to Denmark. Whether things go well or badly, I must go home, alive or dead. Rotting up here, far from my twin, would be the worst thing after all. I put the four cartridges in my pocket and set out into the twilight. My fatigue has lifted. My body is prepared for one last, decisive exertion.

Ghost Landscape

Thin as matchsticks, bereft of needles, and painted white with frost, the larch trees spread out around me like a huge labyrinth. I allow my eyes to wander back and forth between the trunks. Nothing moves, not the slightest sign of life anywhere. The taiga is cold and lifeless. I feel as if I am moving through a deep, dead silence. With my gun on my back, I climb up into a dead tree to get a better view. My hands stiffen on the slippery, icy branches, and the snow falls onto my neck. There is nothing to see, no life-saving moose tracks, nothing. I jump down from the tree and find myself standing in snow up to my ankles.

Once more, I feel despondent and utterly powerless. I start feeling the hunger again. After only an hour, I take a break, light a fire, and boil water. The tea is long gone, but the hot water helps keep the cold away and gives my stomach a sense of fullness. When I look down, I spot a ruby-red shimmer through the snow. Cranberries! I take my glove off, run my fingers through the snow and grab a handful of berries. When I put them in my mouth, they quickly thaw out on my tongue and soften up. The taste is slightly bitter but refreshing, and they give me a sense of renewed energy.

When hunters talk about the Omulevka River, they use it to designate the entire enormous delta formed by the river and its many branches and tributaries. I step out onto one such tributary and walk, slightly hunched over, across the ice, all the while testing the bearing capacity of the frozen surface with my ski pole. Venturing out onto the Siberian rivers can be deadly dangerous. Even if they freeze hard, local streams and warm springs may result in thin spots. Once you fall into the cold water, it is only a matter of seconds before your muscles cramp up. Then you are done for.

Once I have reached about one-third of the way across the river, I hear a loud crack and feel the ice starting to collapse underneath my feet. I increase my speed, but the bank is still far away, and the ice is cracking faster than I can run.

In desperation, I reach into my pocket, pull out one of the cartridges, and throw it down into one of the many cracks, yelling, "This is yours!"

The ice instantly stops cracking, as if held together by an invisible force, and I reach the bank without so much as wetting my feet. I recall "Grandma" Akulina in Nelemnoye, who told me, along with lots of other pieces of good advice, how to make offerings to the forest, the lakes, and the rivers: "Just a coin or some other bits and pieces. That's enough." I may have lost a precious cartridge, but all the same I feel that is what saved my life.

The landscape on the opposite bank of the river turns out to be a dreary and somber place. The riverbank here is flat and flooded during the summer. The water relentlessly eats into the forest, draining all of its vigor. Now, only dead and half-dead trees are left, overgrown with a frizzy layer of gray lichen. They are like a reflection of my own weakened state, and the farther I make my way into this dead forest, the drearier the whole scenario seems. In this ghostly landscape, I feel like a ghost myself, walking among remnants of a life that has long since expired. My shoulder strikes a branch, breaking it and knocking down a shower of dust and mold.

At the same instant, I hear a deep grunt to my right. I turn around and see the contours of a large shadow hidden behind some tall willow shrubs 150 feet away. My heart sinks. The bear! I start to back away, terrified that it will see me.

But my fear is brief, replaced by a sudden decisiveness. "Whatever the hell it is, it's got to die, or we'll starve to death." I load the rifle with the last three cartridges and note that the wind direction is right. Then I push my skis off my feet and start slowly sneaking up on my prey. It is still impossible to see what kind of animal is standing behind the bush. The branches are too dense, and the sun is too low in the sky to provide a proper view.

When I am about thirty feet away, I take a chance and shoot. A cloud of snow rises when the animal falls to the ground. But shortly after that, I catch another glimpse of a raised back, and I shoot two more times. The silence returns; the taiga's abysmal stillness descends again. I am overwhelmed by an immense sense of calm—a sort of comfortable dullness that I do not resist. I fling down the gun and let myself fall back into the snow. The darkness has thickened. I feel no hunger. Rather, I feel comfortably empty. I shift my gaze up and see a firmament sprinkled with stars, glimmering and trembling as if they were sparkling eyes. I have never seen a sky so open and star-spangled, and yet so icy cold. A grave-like calm has fallen, and I let it engulf me.

The Forest's Sacrifice

I lie there for another minute or so, gazing at the stars, but then I start feeling the raw cold in my limbs anew and sit up. The sun has practically disappeared behind the horizon. I can only just make out the shrubbery that I fired my last rounds into. It will soon be pitch-dark and impossible to find my bearings. I gather my strength and drag myself to the spot, where I am finally rewarded: a cow moose and its calf are lying dead in the snow. More than thirteen hundred pounds of dead meat is lying before me. I laugh to myself. From the cow's bulging udder, rich, creamy milk is flowing. I instantly start to feel hungry, put my mouth to the udder, and drink in heavy gulps. Life stirs anew in my every fiber.

"So this was what last night's dream foretold: the woman and child in my dream were the cow and calf sacrificing their lives so that Ivan and I can go on living," I think. "Grandma" Akulina once explained to me that "hunting is the same as making love."[3] Only now do I understand what she meant. I get up and lower my head in respect for the dead animals.

Then I open their stomachs to prevent them from rotting. I have neither the time nor the strength to carve them up properly. I cut a chunk off the cow's hind leg, swallow a couple of hefty bites of the raw meat and put the rest in my backpack. But my stomach has been empty for too long and cannot handle such hefty fare, so I begin to vomit.

"We'll have to start with soup," I think, covering both carcasses with snow. Hopefully that will keep them out of sight of the predators until I can return and build a rack.

■　■　■

Most of the trip back to the cabin takes place in complete darkness. I cannot see my skis, not even the white snow, nothing. And on top of that, the cold has taken hold of my hands, which are wet with blood. I take off my mittens and warm them under my armpits. After a few minutes, I regain sufficient sensation in my fingers to hold the ski pole again. Stepping carefully, I feel my way forward in my old tracks, which eventually lead me home. Cold, my knees and back battered, I throw myself onto the bunk, fully dressed, and fall asleep.

The following day, I wake up late, dazed by the hardships of the day before. I look over at Ivan, lying on his bunk, watching the pot steaming with moose meat soup. He turns toward me and sends me a little thank-you glance with his eyes. The first spoonful is wonderful, and the next is even better. In fact, neither of us has ever tasted such a good meal, despite the fact that we have neither salt nor other spices, and that the soup is just a pot of boiled water with chunks of fat in it. We feel our bodies immediately regaining some of their lost strength.

It feels good to be human. The survival instinct that has consumed us for so long shrinks as our stomachs fill up, and we suddenly hear ourselves laughing. Ivan pulls out two crumpled cigarettes. He has been saving them for a special occasion, and before long we are lying there, blowing smoke up at the ceiling, slapping our stomachs.

We are both tired after starving for a long time, but we have also learnt from our mistake, so the very next day I go back to the moose meat to build a rack. Luckily, the meat is untouched. I remove the branches from three larch trees, standing five or six feet apart, forming a triangle. On top, about twelve feet off the ground, I build a platform for the meat. I place a decent pile of willow twigs under the meat, allowing about two feet of branches to jut out all around the platform. This is to stop the wolverine climbing up there. I cover the meat with the moose hides, so that the ravens cannot get to it either. As a final precaution, I place three large traps with jagged jaws at the foot of the rack.

"Now you can just try it, wolverine!" I grumble sarcastically and head for home.

■ ■ ■

A week later, we suddenly hear the sound of snowmobiles. At first, it is just a faint hum, but it soon becomes quite clear. There is no doubt. I am setting up a sable trap quite far from the cabin, but I throw the trap aside and race back to find Yura and Sinitskiy sitting on the bunk next to Ivan. It has been almost two and half months since we last saw each other.

"What the hell is this I'm hearing?" Yura laughs and hugs me. "You've been starving to death. What a pair of amateurs." Yura and Sinitskiy start eating some of the moose meat while Ivan and I dig into the cookies, candy, and cigarettes they have brought. It is a blessing of flavors and pure delight after being in the clutches of starvation for such a long time.

The news from Nelemnoye is not good. The police are still looking for me, and Shadrin has vanished from the face of the earth. So far, nobody knows where he is. The hunters have lost faith in the fur project and have decided to hand over their next catch to Sakhabult.

We decide that Ivan, who is still troubled by his foot, should go back to Nelemnoye with Sinitskiy and the sack of around forty sable furs. I will travel west with Yura and the dogs toward Spiridon and his hunting group. I have started getting used to life in the taiga and am looking forward to finally being in the company of real Yukaghir hunters.

7

I FLING MY BACKPACK OFF the snowmobile and step into Spiridon's log cabin. It is very similar to the one Ivan and I were living in but is much more spacious and better equipped. And it is situated in the middle of the Omulevka Delta, with a large open hunting area around it. Everything is bigger and better than where I have come from.

The men's sleeping bags lie neatly rolled together on the bunks, which are covered with moose fur. And the joints in the wall are sealed so that we are not exposed to drafts. In the middle of the room is a wide table, affixed to the wall, and around it two long benches and a stool. Here the men are sitting eating. The firewood beside the stove is systematically stacked along the wall, from floor to ceiling. There is also a metal plate of dry wood shavings so that the hunter who sleeps closest to the stove does not need to get out of his sleeping bag to light the fire in the morning. Crawling out of your sleeping bag in a cold cabin is not exactly a pleasure. In particular, sticking your feet down into frozen boots is a real pain. So you light the fire while you are lying in your sleeping bag.

Close to the door, farthest from the stove, the men's reindeer-skin boots and socks are hanging to dry, each on its own nail. Wet fur must not be exposed to intense heat, because then it dries out and splits. Along the other beams of the cabin, various spare parts from rifles, snowmobiles, and chainsaws are hanging. Even plastic bags, tin cans, and nylon string have been hung up. Nothing is thrown away but is kept for later use. And the roof of the cabin is cleverly

Spiridon Spiridonov's hunting cabin.   103

Hunter's boots and socks, both made of reindeer skin. The soles of the boots are covered with the hairs from between the reindeer's hooves. Drawing by Sara Heil Jensen.

built to provide space for an extra room, where supplies are stored. It is high and steep to prevent bears reaching the storeroom or breaking into the log cabin itself through the ceiling. Clearly, I have come to a well-organized cabin, where thought has been given to even the smallest details.

My expectations are high when I meet this living legend Spiridon. I had imagined a chieftain type: erect and muscular with high cheekbones and an aquiline nose. But instead, standing in front of me is a short, skinny man with broad jaws, flat nose, and parchment-thin skin. In a dry, almost whining tone, he welcomes me to the camp, after which he gives orders to his youngest son, Peter, to boil water for tea. Spiridon's oldest son, Yura, is free from housework, which is always assigned to the youngest in the hunting party. Actually, at twenty-seven I am a full four years younger than Peter, but I have special status as a newly arrived guest and am not ordered around.

We drink dark, Gruzian tea with sugar, and Yura explains my situation and why I am here to his father. However, Spiridon does not show any special interest in the fur project or the political crisis it has caused. His world is the forest and the moose. Who buys furs from whom and for what price are remote and unimportant to him. Spiridon has spent the seventy-six years of his life in the forests around the River Omulevka. He only rarely appears in the village. The density of buildings and the many smells of people and garbage are said to have a suffocating effect on him.

"Spiridon's favorite company," Grandmother Akulina tells me, "is the owner of the River Omulevka." By this, she means the spirit who provides him with large numbers of moose out of love for him.

Sauna in the Tent

Yura continues his account of my hardships, but Spiridon interrupts him: "Tomorrow we'll go out and see the Big One. Pitch the tent so that we can be cleansed. The Big One doesn't like the smell of human sweat."

Neither Yura nor Peter protests. They immediately get up, go out, and erect a canvas tent in front of the cabin. Meanwhile, I go down to the river and chop flakes off the three-foot-thick ice with a long wooden spear with a hefty metal spike on the end, and then bring the ice up to the tent in buckets.

The water from the melted ice boils. All four of us sit naked in the tent, and Spiridon repeatedly throws the water on the glowing stove. The deadly heat almost knocks me out. It feels as if boiling water is being poured down my back, and I have difficulty breathing. Yura passes me a bunch of dried birch twigs, which he has dipped in hot water: "Breathe through them."

When we are completely flushed and bathed in sweat, we lie on our stomachs one by one, and then Spiridon flogs our bodies with birch twigs until we look like streaky bacon.

"The Big One loves the sweet smell of birch and will not be shy but will come to meet us," Yura says, lifting up the tent flap to roll out into the snow.

■ ■ ■

"Spiridon is the name of the man who never takes time to sleep or rest. As long as there are mouths to feed, he looks for moose both day and night. With sunken eyes and dry mouth, he continues his hunt until he falls over in exhaustion. When that happens, hunger sets in." This is how Akulina described Spiridon the first time I asked about the man who feeds most of the population of the village through his hunting. If the locals' stories are to be believed, Spiridon is an extraordinary pursuer of moose. Once, he is said to have shooed a big bull moose into the hunting camp as if it were a tame cow, where it collapsed of exhaustion right in front of the fire.

In the frost, the steam rises from Yura's body as from a boiling kettle.

"Wouldn't some soap be preferable to being beaten up like that?" I groan, flinging myself into the salvation of the cold snow.

"Are you mad? Everything that smells of humans, be it soap, alcohol, or sex, is banned when it comes to meeting the Big One." Yura is on his knees, rubbing his body with snow.

"Who the hell actually is the Big One?" I ask, now pretty tired of being frozen after first being boiled up.

"Shhh!" Yura whispers. "He can hear us. That's what we call the moose when we're out to get him, so he doesn't know that he's the one we're looking for."

I am too cold and exhausted to ask further questions. So I totter back to the cabin, where I throw myself down into my sleeping bag and fall into a deep sleep.

The Moose Sacrifices Itself

In the morning, we are woken in true military fashion by Spiridon going around banging with a ladle on an old pan.

"Wake up, lazybones! There's work to be done," he croaks in his dry old man's voice. Yura is already sitting on the edge of the bunk, putting his trousers on. Peter, like myself, has only just woken up and is lying rubbing his eyes. To Spiridon's credit, it must be said that he has already gotten everything ready. The stove is roaring, and the old, sooty pot of boiled meat is standing steaming on the table. It will be a long day of work, so we have to eat up. The others are already sitting with their long knives, cutting the pieces of meat off right next to their teeth.

"Did you see anything?" mumbles Yura with his mouth full of meat, looking over at Spiridon.

"Yes, I visited her last night. The Big One is coming to meet us." Spiridon puts a beautifully embroidered fur coat and hood on. Before he slams the door behind him, he shouts, "Get a move on! We've got to get going."

"What on earth were you talking about?" I ask Yura.

Yura thinks for a moment. "How should I explain it to you?" Then he reaches down into Spiridon's sleeping bag and pulls out a little wooden figurine. It has the shape of a crudely carved human body, with lines marking eyes, nose, and mouth. Something resembling moose antlers have been carved on top of the head.

"This is my father's *ayibii,* or what the Russians call a soul (Russian, *dusha*)," Yura explains. "During the night, it goes to the owner of the River Omulevka. She lives in a house with a big stall. All the animals live there—when they're not running round in the forest, that is. She loves Dad, and they have . . ." Yura stops for a moment and laughs. Peter laughs with him.

"What?" I ask impatiently.

"Well, they have sex with each other."

"But why do they do that?" I am quite dumbfounded.

"Because then the Big One comes running all by herself."

"I don't understand a damned thing," I mutter, throwing my rifle over my shoulder.

"No, I thought not," says Yura. "But you'll see it all today, and then maybe you'll understand."

■ ■ ■

We have walked for four hours on short, broad skis whose sliding surfaces are covered with the leg skin (Russian, *kamus*) of a moose. This counteracts slipping backwards and makes it possible for us to go uphill, even in slippery snow. Spiridon points to a track in the snow. He does not say anything but signals that we are to stand still. He himself continues out into a clearing some few yards farther forward. He waddles back and forth on his skis, and his body has taken a new shape. He no longer appears like an ordinary man. The fur jacket worn with its hair turned outwards, the fur hood with tassels of moose ears sewn on, and the fur-covered skis all make his movements look rather like those of a moose. And yet his human nose, eyes, and mouth can be glimpsed under his hood. In his hands he holds his loaded rifle.

Suddenly a cow moose steps out of the brush, along with her lean, long-legged calf. At first the two animals stand still, while the mother

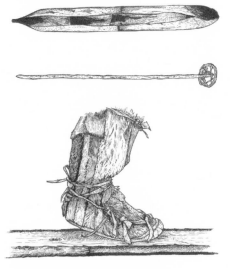

Skiing equipment. Drawings by Marie Carsten Pedersen.

Hunter's hood and clothing
made from reindeer skin with
the fur turned out. Drawings
by Sara Heil Jensen.

lifts her enormous head with its long, pointed beard up and down in
evident confusion about what kind of being is approaching. But as
Spiridon gets closer, she is seized by his movements, sets her mistrust
aside, and runs straight toward him, with the calf bounding
after her. In the same instant, Spiridon lifts his rifle and kills
both of them with a volley of four shots.

I stand gaping as I watch the whole scene, which seems
completely crazy. Yura nudges me in the side: "That's what I
said, the Big One comes all by herself."

"Well . . . ," I mutter, but I can't think of anything to say.

Spiridon beckons us over to the site of the kill. Peter has
carved a little wooden figurine, which Spiridon sprinkles
with blood from the animals and hangs up by a thin thread
above the carcasses.

"There's the murderer," says Yura, pointing to the figurine. "It was him, and not us, who killed the Big One, and the
owner of the River Omulevka will punish him." Yura laughs.

"Yeah, why not . . . ," I mutter, beginning to cut the belly
of the calf open.

Wooden figurine of the "animal killer."
Drawing by Marie Carsten Pedersen.

Animals Are Humans in Disguise

Everything I have seen and heard in the past few days has given me a new insight into the hunters' world—an insight that decisively overturns my preconception of hunting as something fundamentally violent. It is a widespread perception among anthropologists that hunting has played a decisive role in human evolution. In fact, several researchers assert that we humans have become who we are—with our superior intellect, our group behavior, and our ability to produce and use tools—as a direct result of the fact that our forefathers took up hunting.

"Hunting has dominated human history," write the anthropologists Sherwood Washburn and Chet Lancaster in one of the most influential articles in evolutionary theory. "Our intellect, interests, emotions, and basic social life—all are evolutionary products of the success of the hunting adaptation."[1] But there was also a price to pay, the argument goes: as hunters, we developed a "killer instinct" and became violent and brutal by nature. So it is not a coincidence that our history is extremely gory, from the Incas' human sacrifices to the Nazis' mass murder. All this brutality is grounded in our deep-rooted killer instinct, which was developed tens of thousands of years ago in connection with making hunting a way of life.[2]

The theory outlined here is known as "the hunting hypothesis" and has had enormous influence, not just among anthropologists but also in popular culture, from short stories and cartoon strips to films and television, where, as we know, the primeval hunter is typically depicted as a savage who brutally beat every living thing to death with his club. But although hunting by its nature involves a killing, I have begun to question how much actual evidence exists to draw a direct connection between hunting and human brutality. Is the fact that our forefathers became hunters really the reason that our history has had such a violent course?

There is not much evidence to be had when I consider Spiridon and his hunting group. They regard hunting as a fundamentally nonviolent activity, in which the moose, out of sexual desire or rather love for the hunter, virtually sacrifices itself to them. Among many experienced hunters in my own part of the world, one can find corresponding ideas about the prey animal as a kind of love object. A hunter expressed this sentiment to the author John Mitchell: "There is tremendous sexuality in this [hunting] . . . in the sense of wanting something deeply, in the sense of *eros*."[3] The empathy for prey, which for the hunter can easily lead to actual feelings of affection, also emerges time and again in hunting literature from the Middle Ages to today, where the hunter simply falls in love with the animals he kills.[4]

Perhaps the real evolutionary outcome of humans taking up hunting is not a violent and brutal killer instinct but rather the ability to empathize with other beings, an attempt to put oneself in the animal's place and see the world from its perspective. This empathy is reflected in the cosmological principle found among indigenous hunting peoples from the Amazon to North America and Siberia. The Brazilian anthropologist Eduardo Viveiros de Castro calls it "perspectivism."[5] Like the Arawete and other Amazonian groups described by Viveiros de Castro, the Yukaghirs regard the subjectivity of humans and nonhumans as formally the same, because they share the same kinds of souls, *ayibii,* which provide them with a similar or identical perspective or viewpoint on the world. Nonhumans—animals, trees, spirits, and inanimate objects—thus see the world as humans do: they live in households and kin groups similar to those of humans, and see themselves as human beings moving around the landscape, hunting for their animal prey.

Indeed, as the Russian anthropologist Waldemar Bogoras writes, every being, even "the shadows on the wall constitute definitive tribes and have their own country, where they live in huts and subsist by hunting."[6] What differentiates the various species' perspectives from one another is the materiality of the body: human beings see the moose as prey, because human beings share the same kind of body, to the same extent that the moose, with its particular body, sees the human hunter as a cannibal spirit or predator that wants to kill and eat it. In other words, it is bodies that see and determine what is seen; who you are and how you perceive and construct the world all depend on the kind of body you have. This is why shamanism and hunting in Siberia so often involve dressing in hides or by other means exchanging bodies with animals.[7]

It is also in relation to this universe of human-animal transformations that Spiridon's hunting technique must be understood. By transforming himself in the image of the moose, he comes to see the world as the animal sees it, and that provides advantages when he has to lure the animal to him and kill it. However, the danger of undergoing a complete transformation is always present, and so you have to be vigilant when you transform yourself into an animal like this. There are several accounts of hunters who never return to their original human form but go on living with the animals. Stories of this kind are not always just myths but may also be based on personal experiences.

An elderly hunter told me how he had once been out hunting wild reindeer, which was the Yukaghirs' most important prey animal until the moose migrated into the area in large numbers in the 1970s. He had followed a small group of about ten head of reindeer for a couple of days and was thoroughly exhausted and hungry. On a ridge, he suddenly saw an old man, who beckoned to him. The man was dressed in the traditional Yukaghir garb with open jacket and leather apron. When the hunter asked the old man who he was, he did not answer but signaled with his hand that he was to follow him.

While they walked, the hunter wondered at the fact that the old man left tracks of reindeer hooves instead of skis. But he ignored it, thinking that he was hungry and tired and so must be hallucinating. They came to a large camp where there were children running around, playing, and old people sitting in front of their tents, smoking pipes. The old man led him into his tent, where, to his great surprise, he was served reindeer lichen instead of meat. But when he tasted the lichen, it actually tasted like juicy reindeer meat. Even more surprising was the fact that his hosts grunted to each other instead of speaking in a human language. He began to forget basic things such as the names of his own wife and children.

When he lay down to sleep, he heard an inner voice say, "You don't belong here. Run away!" That made the hunter pull himself together, and while his hosts were asleep, he sneaked out of the tent and went back to Nelemnoye.[8]

The people the hunter had met were reindeer, who in their own land take human form, and he himself had been frighteningly close to transforming into one of them. He finished his story by saying that if he had known, he would have killed them and brought their meat back to the village. But the Yukaghirs' idea that animals are really humans in disguise presents a profound moral problem: in a way, they behave like cannibals when they sink their teeth into a piece of animal flesh that conceals a human soul, and this is particularly true for people, like the Yukaghirs, who live almost exclusively from hunting.[9] So it may not be coincidental that many of the Yukaghirs' myths deal with this dilemma of plotting to take the life of an animal, which is in fact a human in disguise. "Life as a hunter is a sinful existence," I have heard several of the older Yukaghirs say. This manifests itself most clearly in the case of the bear. Thus, I have met several Yukaghirs who refuse to eat bear meat on the grounds that bears are too much like humans, and so to eat them would be a kind of cannibalism.

What Do Animals Think?

This idea that humans and animals are not essentially different, that animals can do things that greatly resemble what humans can do, is not as foreign as one might think. A series of ethological studies have attempted to understand the world from the animal's perspective. They have proven that animals, particularly the larger mammals such as dolphins, elephants, and apes, possess language, intentionality, and self-awareness, and they possess these traits to such an extent that the widely accepted boundary between human and animal, subject and object, has become blurred.[10]

For example, if we examine language, which more than anything else has demarcated human from animal, it turns out that apes can in fact learn to construct quite complex sentences with the aid of human sign language. In the same way, studies have proven that certain apes can invent new knowledge and transmit it between generations. This is the case among a group of monkeys that have taught themselves to wash potatoes before they eat them. Thus, these monkeys do not just eat the potatoes as an automatic response to hunger, they also wash the food so that it tastes better. In the terminology of the famous French anthropologist Claude Lévi-Strauss, the monkeys have thereby crossed the boundary between "raw" and "cooked," between "nature" and "culture."[11]

It is unclear, however, how much insight these ethological studies really give us into how animals think and see the world. One of the problems with the studies is that they cannot avoid using humankind as a yardstick when they attempt to demonstrate that animals can do things that resemble what we do, such as communicating in language. The result is that animals are seen as incomplete humans. But an ape is not an incomplete human, it is a complete ape, and so it is understandably not as good as us at behaving like a human or learning our language.[12] We could reverse the experiment and investigate whether we can learn to speak the ape's language. After all, if we are actually at a higher stage of development than the ape, it should be quite easy for us to learn to speak like an ape. But we cannot, precisely because we are humans.[13]

In reality perhaps the studies tell us less about how animals think and perceive the world, and more about the limits of our own human powers of imagination. Ultimately, we cannot see the world with eyes other than our purely human ones. We can only see what our own human frame of reference permits us to see. Perhaps this is precisely what the Yukaghirs have realized when they claim that animals see the world as we do, that is, as humans. This point is echoed in American philosopher Thomas Nagel's famous essay "What Is It Like to Be a Bat?" in which he wrote that even though the bat's sonar is a form of perception, it is not comparable with anything humans possess, and there is no reason to think that it is something we can experience or imagine.[14] Our own experience is the basis for our imagination, and so its breadth is limited.

Does this mean that we will never come to understand what animals actually think? Yes, it probably does. But what I find insightful is that the quote above justifies an anthropomorphic approach to animals in a certain sense, that is, attributing human characteristics to animals out of a desire to understand them. For example, if we cannot say that an animal is "sad" or "happy," then what can we say about it? Nothing at all. Without a certain humanization of the animal, we are not in a position to understand or describe its world. So even if we may regard the humanization of animals as sentimental and unscientific, it is necessary if we are to create an understanding of animals that reaches beyond the purely mechanical notion of the animal as a biological being. Besides, humanization also serves an ethical function: If we do not entertain notions that animals in some sense think like us, then what would bring us to discuss whether it is reasonable for us to subject them to experiments, put them in cages, or hunt them? It is precisely because the Yukaghirs in their myths regard animals as humans in disguise that they never stop questioning whether it is ethically defensible to live from killing and eating animals.

Ice Fishing

"What about setting up a fishing net down on the river?" Yura suggests, quickly pulling a rolled-up net down from the beam under the ceiling. Peter goes along with the idea. "Fish is excellent bait for the sable traps, and I'm fed up with moose meat," he says.

But set up a fishing net? After all, the river and lakes are covered in ice three feet thick. How could it be possible? I look inquiringly from one to the other. Yura and Peter laugh. "It's hard work, but it's certainly possible to drag a net under the ice," Yura assures me.

We get to work chopping holes in the ice of a small lake. I still do not grasp what is to happen, and Peter explains while we slave away with our spikes. "The holes should be in a straight line, and the distance between the first and last should be the same as the length of the net. When the holes are ready, we tie a rope to the end of a tree trunk and pass it in under the ice through the first hole. The tree trunk is then pushed from hole to hole so that the rope is passed on to the last hole in the row. One end of the fishing net is tied to the rope and the net can now be dragged under the ice by pulling the rope from the other end."

The net is usually checked only every second day, but we cannot wait, and check it for catch the next morning. Yura has tied the rope to one end of the net, and Peter and I are in the process of pulling it up from the opposite end. It is heavy—there is a catch, lots of juicy fish!

A moment later, I have to stick my frozen-blue fingers in my mouth. I look enviously at the two hunters. The ice-cold water does not seem to bother them in the least. With amazing speed, they wrest the fish out of the net and throw their more or less lifeless bodies into a big sack.

"Sucking your thumb doesn't help!" Yura laughs, throwing a flapping pike at my head. He orders me to gut it so that we can have something to eat.

"But there's no firewood out here," I protest.

"Firewood!" Yura sneers. He takes a firm grip of one of the fish, cuts its head off and takes a bite of the raw fish.

I watch his contented chomping with a feeling of nausea.

"You'd better get started if you don't want to go to bed hungry," Yura growls, pulling a bone out of the corner of his mouth.

Full of loathing, I sink my teeth into the fish. Its flesh is porous but actually does not taste all that bad.

Now I realize that the fishing net is the hunter's most important tool, more important than the rifle. When Ivan and I were starving, we were not aware that food was swimming around just outside our cabin. Instead I went out on one exhausting meat hunt after the other. As I learned for myself the hard way, the taiga can be completely devoid of life. You can wander for weeks without seeing the shadow of prey. But with the fishing net, you can catch food for yourself and your dogs and get the necessary bait for the traps. The fishing net is, you might say, the hunter's life insurance.

Hunter Heart and Soul

The days almost fly by and quickly become weeks and months. Moose are shot, firewood is chopped, and traps are set. Every day is a physical toil, but never before have I felt such undaunted enthusiasm for my scope and freedom. I am totally absorbed in the deserted and enigmatic nature of the taiga. Every morning I go out with the same indomitable desire to expose it: What is hiding behind the next crest or ravine, a moose, a sable, or nothing? I do not know in advance, but my curiosity is the same every day, and it drives me on. It is the hunter's curiosity that has now become part of my innermost being, as the taiga has become my home, my whole universe.

I have gradually learned many of the tricks of hunting life. I have learned to find my way in the forest with the aid of the North Star. With a branch I can imitate a rutting bull moose scratching its antlers with passion and strength against a tree trunk. Nobody could guess that a human is making that sound. I can howl like a wolf, and it is not just the cubs that answer me but also the adult wolves. Not to mention the white grouse, which I can call to me without difficulty.

During the night, I am sometimes visited in my dreams by the young black-haired woman I saw while starving, who gives me a coin or a piece of bread and butter or makes love to me. The coin indicates that I will encounter a sable; the bread, a hare or white grouse; and the sex, a moose. It works virtually every time. I have finally incorporated all facets of the hunter's life into my own physical and spiritual existence. And still I am surprised. Yet again my preconceptions of the life of the hunter are turned upside down.

During a hunt with Yura, we come across a moose track, and he asks me to tell him which direction the animal has gone. I bend down and look at the track in the snow. It is not difficult to decipher. Small beads of snow have been pushed forward to the right of the track, and that shows the direction of the moose quite clearly.

I say this self-confidently to Yura, who to my surprise replies, "Wrong!"

I look again at the track but reach the same conclusion.

"No," he replies in an authoritative voice, without so much as looking at the track.

This strange conversation continues for half a minute, and I eventually become quite unsure of my own ability.

Then Yura suddenly smiles and says, "Don't be sad. I was only testing you. Remember never to let anybody tell you what's right and wrong. Each hunter must say, 'Only I know what's right!'"

At first I do not understand the intention of Yura's behavior, but later I realize that it is symptomatic of the logic of the hunters. In their world you must never accept what people tell you without first investigating the matter yourself. This does not mean that you should refuse to listen to what other people have to say, or keep what you know to yourself. On the contrary, knowledge about hunting is considered to be collective property among the Yukaghirs, so a hunter is obliged to say what he knows.[15] But for the individual hunter, knowledge is only knowledge when he himself has tested and experienced it in practice. Like many other Arctic peoples, the Yukaghirs do not regard information as real knowledge until a person has experienced the matter for himself.[16] Firsthand knowledge is an absolute precondition for knowing anything at all.

This may seem strange to those of us who give great weight to linguistic communication in practically all aspects of life, from school and work to the private sphere, where we feel we have understood each other only when we have spoken to each other. But recent cognitive research—the generic term for research drawing on psychology, computer science, and linguistics in the development of theories about human perception, thinking, and learning—has demonstrated that most of our knowledge is in fact nonlinguistic and that this knowledge is transmitted most efficiently in ways that bypass language.[17]

If we go back to my reading of the animal track, the knowledge I used can hardly have a linear, logical form, as is the case with our language. If it had such a form, I would not be able to explain the speed and efficiency with which I performed the task. It took me only a split second to read the track. But when I had to explain to Yura how I decoded the track, the task suddenly became extraordinarily complicated and awkward.

The Test of Manhood
At the end of March, a new season is in the making. The weather changes to a mild thaw, which is brought to the taiga by a warm southwesterly wind. The snow, which collapses due to the humidity, turns into a hard, slippery shell of ice in the morning hours, before

the sun warms it up. These conditions are a real nightmare for the moose, which because of its heavy weight bores deep down into the snow, so its legs are cut by the sharp ice edges and bleed, but are ideal for the hunter, who slides on his skis quickly and lightly over the glassy surface.

I am out hunting with Yura and Peter. Spiridon has left the camp for a week, which happens often. He does not tolerate human company for long at a time, preferring to explore the forest on his own. It is completely clear and frosty and so blindingly bright that we cannot look at the glittering mirror of the snow without sunglasses. On a wide, frozen meadow, we pass a fresh moose track. The animal's hooves have splintered the icy surface as if it were glass. The tracks are very deep and continue across the meadow and over a treeless ridge.

"Will we go after it?" I ask eagerly. Yura shakes his head. I look at the track again and am inclined to agree with him. The tracks have been made with hooves lifted high, which shows quite clearly that the animal is at the peak of its strength. When the moose is fatigued, long semicircles appear around the holes in the snow, left as it swings its legs out to the side in exhaustion.

We are about to move on when I suddenly stop and burst out, "Let me try to catch up with it. I know I can do it." The words seem to shoot out of my mouth. I do not know why, but I feel myself loaded with an almost unreal strength, and my confidence is unlimited.

I have never before felt so bursting with energy. This is possibly because of our diet, which may have been a little monotonous—moose or fish for every meal of the day—but always in abundant quantities, but mostly because I have now begun to feel experienced enough to make decisions for myself and because I see an opportunity for action in the landscape. Yes, it is as if the landscape directly demands that I act.

At first Yura gives me a skeptical look. He is about to refuse but then sees my wildly blazing eyes and changes his mind. With a brief nod, I get his permission, and the hunt gets started.

There is more at stake than just bagging a moose for the sake of the meat. Now I must prove to him and the others that I have completed my apprenticeship, that I am no longer a boy or an unadjusted foreigner but a man and a hunter of the taiga. Now I will prove that I can kill a moose when I want to.

■   ■   ■

I follow the tracks at a light run across the meadow and up onto the treeless ridge. Here the landscape has an entirely different complexion, an entirely different shape from the terrain I know in the lowland. It is a frozen and barren wilderness, where the wind has curled up the snow into frozen folds, as if fossilized.

The tracks continue toward the opposite ridge, and I follow them at a fast pace. I cross another ridge and another. The dry wind cuts into my lungs, and my earflaps, eyebrows, and lashes get covered in frost. But even in this murderous wind, which makes my lungs cramp up, and where every second I have to bring the blood back to my frozen cheeks and nose by rubbing them with the fur on my mittens, I feel the need to discharge all my physical reserves. The moose must be caught, and I keep running along the track.

The animal is clearly suffering in the hard frozen snow, as here and there I see torn-off tufts of hair from its shins, and later dark red stripes of blood. The icy crust of snow has compelled it to reduce its pace, and that gives me a chance to gain on it.

Finally, after two hours' pursuit, I see the moose in the distance. A large, magnificent bull. Its legs are pinned into the snow like stiff posts. With its heavily laden antlers, it looks monumental, almost as if it were carved in granite. I am about 150 yards from it, still too far away to be able to shoot. So I continue toward it.

Suddenly it turns its head, directs its long ears toward me, and sniffs. It has noticed me. It snorts excitedly, and steam comes out of its nostrils. Then it leaps out to the side and sets off at a fast run.

Mittens, lined with hare fur and edged with fox fur. Drawing by Sara Heil Jensen.

Desperate, I put the rifle to my cheek and fire off two shots, both of which miss. I am so out of breath, I cannot hold the gun steady at all.

I am on the brink of giving up the chase when I realize that the moose is on its way toward yet another ridge. If I get there in time, I will be able to shoot it on its way up the slope. As if flung from a catapult, I continue my run. I can hardly breathe, and I can feel how my knees are about to give way. But I keep sprinting and just manage to see the moose throwing its enormous body forward toward the top of the hill. So it is now or never. I lift the rifle to fire and hold my breath. My eyes, which are stuck together by frost, blink feverishly to get a view. But shoot I do. Twice.

The moose sinks to its knees with a heavy rattle, as if it has acknowledged what has happened, and then rolls down the hill, where its gigantic, lifeless body lands on a rocky outcrop. A current of warmth streams through my exhausted chest, and I hear myself give a triumphant howl of joy. However, my body is still quivering with excitement and cold, so I stay standing in the same spot, still gasping for air. But I know what is to be done, and after a short rest I go over to the moose, slit its belly open, and pull the stomach out. There are no trees on the barren plain, so I cannot carve a miniature of the "murderer," as tradition demands. Instead I cut the animal's long, black beard off. This is said to have the same protective effect against attack from its "owner." Then I make my way back to the others.

"Well, what's up?" Yura asks casually when I find him and Peter sitting drinking tea.

I cannot restrain my feeling of victory and almost shout, "I bloody well did it! It's lying four ridges away."

Yura looks at me in amazement, as if he cannot quite figure out whether I am mocking him. But when it is clear that I have really bagged the moose, he snarls casually, "How the hell do you think we're to fetch the meat and bring it back to the cabin?"

But his harsh words are one thing, and his eyes are another, sparkling with joy and respect. Peter also nods approvingly and smiles.

Perhaps my sense of victory is really something irresistible and there exists a recognition that I have earned it at that moment. In any case, they both clearly acknowledge that I have been able to handle something that they did not think I could do. A worthy reward for all my troubles.

8

A LONG-AWAITED FRIEND

THE END OF APRIL brings about some striking events. First, the long-awaited spring arrives. The young bright light grows and becomes warmer and more powerful day by day. In the course of just a week, the temperature rises from minus 22 to 50 degrees. There is certainly still frost at night, but there is a lovely warmth from the sun by day. And along with the warmth come the wild geese, whose wing feathers' sonorous swishing resonates almost constantly through the air. In long, wedge-shaped rows, they fly north to breed on a vast hatching area near the Arctic Ocean.

We place wooden decoys out on the ice and sit hidden in small snow trenches. First a loud singing swish is heard, as if the air is whistling with masses of feathers. Then a flock streaks like a bolt of lightning toward the earth to sit beside what they think are members of their own species. At that instant, we stand up out of our hides and send a shower of shot in over them.

To bag a sitting goose does not require any special skill, but bagging them in flight is difficult and requires practice. Despite their clumsy appearance, geese fly extremely quickly, and in addition you have to know the velocity of the balls of shot and the influence of cross- and headwinds on your shot.

When the bird is flying away from you—at approximately the height of a man—you should aim for its head. When it is flying very high, you should hold the barrel under the bird, and at even greater distance aim for its neck. When the bird is flying low, you should take it right on the foresight, and at low height, aim somewhat higher or in

Gregory Shalugin drives the snowmobile, towing his wife Akulina on the sledge.

Wooden decoys. Drawing by Sara Heil Jensen.

front of the bird. I know all of this only in theory, and I miss one shot after the other.

Spiridon looks at me in resignation, as if he is on the brink of taking the shotgun away from me. But then the rhythm finally begins to take root in my body, and I get my heart to beat calmly before the shot. First I hit a goose that comes flying from the side, and then I hit one that is rising in a straight line over my head. Now I have mastered the art of shooting birds in flight and am not lagging behind the others. From the first ray of sun until the light of day eventually fades away behind the Kolyma Upland mountain range, our shots constantly slash through the still air. When we make our way home to the cabin, we have bagged no fewer than thirty-five geese. Poultry flesh in large amounts. A much-needed change to the menu.

■　■　■

The next morning, as we sit outside the cabin, plucking a small mountain of wild geese, we hear the sound of a snowmobile. At first it is just a faint buzzing, but soon we can hear that it is coming in our direction. Yura orders me into the forest. After all, it may be the police who have resumed pursuit. I quickly gather my things in my backpack, run out among the trees a couple of hundred yards from the cabin, and wait. The snowmobile arrives, the engine is switched off, and I hear Sinitskiy's cheerful voice.

"All clear!" shouts Yura, and I go back to the cabin.

Apart from Sinitskiy, there is another new arrival. He is sitting on the sled, completely wrapped in furs. It is only when he lifts the icy scarf away from his face that I recognize him. Slava Shadrin! I throw out my arms in delighted surprise and embrace him as if he were an old, long-lost friend. He also lights up on seeing me again. In the time that has passed since we last saw each other, more than five months ago, we have gotten significantly closer to each other, probably because we have been thinking about each other constantly.

I have been waiting for news from him, as if he were a shaman, about the state of the fur project, and not least about how long I would have to live as a refugee in the wilderness. For his part, he has been worried that something might have happened to me in the taiga, that I lay dead somewhere in the frost. When we finally find each other alive and well, we both radiate joy. I almost cannot recognize him without his usual reserved and formal manner.

Arrested and Released

In accordance with tradition, the two new arrivals are offered food and drink before we begin to ask for news. But the moment Shadrin pushes the empty plate away, I can no longer control myself, and I almost bombard him with questions: What has happened to the furs? Where has he been for all this time? Are the police still after me?

For a while Shadrin listens, then he nods understandingly and begins to recount the events of the last many months, which turn out to be far more dramatic than I could ever have imagined.

"Shortly after Uffe and you had left for St. Petersburg, I went to Zyryanka to catch a plane to Yakutsk, from where I would send the sable furs to Moscow and then on to Denmark."

Shadrin takes a sip of tea and continues: "There were three members of the police waiting in the airport for me. They said I had broken the law and that they had been ordered to confiscate the sable furs and to take me into custody. I was naturally outraged and asked them to explain the legalities. I also showed them the various permits I had.

"But the police didn't care and didn't even look at the documents. On the whole, they didn't explain themselves in any more detail, but just said that they were acting on orders from the local administration.

"I asked them to write a report of the arrest, so that the event would be made official. They refused. Instead they locked me in jail, and there I overheard one of the policemen calling to inform the district police chief, Irishkhanov, or 'Dudayev' as he calls himself, that everything was now in order. Dudayev has strong connections to Sakhabult, because he formerly worked for Yakutia's ministry of agriculture. I'm convinced that it was Dudayev who had me arrested and the furs confiscated on orders from Petrov."

"Isn't Dudayev the Chechen who invited Uffe home when he came to Zyryanka the first time?" I ask in surprise.

Shadrin nods. "As you know, appearances can be deceptive. Dudayev pretended to be your friend, but he has been in cahoots with Sakhabult the whole time. That's how it is here. It's difficult to distinguish friend from enemy."

I nod in understanding, and Shadrin continues his account.

"I was kept only overnight in jail, then I was released. When I asked about the furs, I was told that they had been transferred to Sakhabult in Yakutsk. I took the next plane to Yakutsk and went directly to Sakhabult's headquarters. Here I met Petrov and his vice president, Anatoliy Maksimov.

"When Petrov saw me, he got very agitated. 'There's the damned Yukaghir! Haven't you had enough?'

"I politely asked to get my sable furs back. But Petrov sneered and explained that only Sakhabult had the right to collect furs, because they were a Yakutian state enterprise.

"I replied that I had all the necessary permits, and that his confiscation of our furs was against Russian federal legislation. Furthermore, I made it plain to him that he was breaking Russia's anti-monopoly legislation by insisting on Sakhabult's exclusive right to handle the republic's furs. Petrov did not reply but snorted in derision and then left the room. He was taking the plane to St. Petersburg, where they were just about to hold a fur auction."

A New Offer

"Meanwhile, the same day that Petrov left Yakutsk, I got a call from the company's vice president, Maksimov, who wanted a meeting with me. He had been totally silent during my row with Petrov, by the way. We met at his office. To my great surprise, he began by admitting that we had the law on our side, and that Petrov was in the wrong in trying to obstruct our trade with Denmark. Furthermore, he explained to me that Sakhabult's monopoly policy was self-destructive, because it forced hunters to sell their best sable furs on the black market, where prices are higher than what Sakhabult is willing to pay. About 25 percent of the hunters' sable furs are thought to go to the black market.

"He suggested that we should cooperate and start a new corporation that would send the republic's sable furs to the auctions in Denmark and pay the hunters a higher price for them. In fact, he explained to me that he was already in the process of having the corporation registered under the name Bulchut, which means 'hunter' in the Sakha language. At the end, he said that I could go down to their freezer room and fetch my sable furs whenever it suited me. Happy about the turn of events, I decided to let the furs stay where they were. I would have to spend some days filling out the customs papers for transport to Denmark anyway, and I thought that the furs were better secured against moths in Sakhabult's freezer compartment than at home in my mother's drafty apartment. But it was too soon to celebrate; my problems were not over.

"When I went back to Sakhabult's headquarters five days later and asked for Maksimov, the guard told me coldly that he was no longer working for the company. When I asked for the furs, I was almost thrown out of the building and told that I was no longer welcome. I have an acquaintance who works for Sakhabult, who later told me that when Petrov came back from the auction and found out that Maksimov had done a deal with me, the two men had come to blows. Maksimov had left Sakhabult with threats to set up his own, competing fur corporation. I thought that I would contact Maksimov but didn't manage it before I read in the paper that he had drowned during a fishing trip with his two sons and that the bodies had not been found."

"Are you saying that Maksimov was murdered?" I interrupt.

Shadrin sighs deeply, as if the incident is too complicated for me to understand, but tries patiently to explain anyway.

"No. Officially, it was a fishing accident. But of course you know yourself how our country works. People are murdered for less than what Maksimov was up to. He was not just anybody. He had personal contacts far up in the top of the Yakutian parliament, Il Tumen, and he must have had support from some powerful people, otherwise he would not have crossed Sakhabult. So he was a serious threat to Sakhabult's fur monopoly.

"You must understand that this is not just a conflict between Sakhabult and us but between different ministries that are fighting with each other for influence. Sakhabult is supported by Yakutia's ministry for agriculture, which functions as a kind of patron for them. In parliament, the ministry for agriculture makes Sakhabult's case. Maksimov and his organization, Bulchut, were supported by Koriakin, who is the head of the republic's association of hunters and fishermen. They are responsible for issuing hunting licenses, among other things. I think Maksimov and Koriakin grew up together and were close friends."

Shadrin pauses briefly before continuing: "We ourselves are supported by Andrey Krivoshapkin, who is the head of the Association of Indigenous Peoples of Yakutia. However, he is mostly a figurehead who has been appointed by the president so that it looks outwardly as if Yakutia is doing something for their indigenous minorities. In reality, he has only little political influence, but he officially supports our fur project. So it's difficult to know who had Maksimov murdered—if he was murdered, that is. In any case, there were several people who would have liked to see him dead. Then again, he could have drowned accidentally. You can die in minutes if you fall into the icy water and help is not at hand.

"When I heard about Maksimov's fate, I became afraid myself. I feared for my own life. For weeks, I moved house and stayed with various friends and acquaintances. However, I kept up contact with Krivoshapkin, who helped me to write a letter to President Vladimir Putin's administration in the Kremlin, in which I explained our situation."

"Vladimir who?" I ask. I seem to have heard the name before but cannot remember the context.

At first Shadrin looks at me in surprise, but then he nods in understanding.

"Oh yes, while you have been out here in the forest, Russia has gotten a new president, Vladimir Putin. He is apparently the diametrical opposite of Boris Yeltsin. Where Yeltsin is irrational, spontaneous, and drunken, Putin is a real KGB technocrat: moderate, cunning, and authoritarian. During the election, he promised zero tolerance for corruption, so I thought that maybe he would support us in our case."

A Favored People

The Yukaghirs' close relationship to power in the Kremlin has always played a special role in their understanding of themselves as a specially favored people in the Russian empire. Under the czar, they were often used as auxiliary soldiers in the struggle against their neighboring peoples, especially the Chukchi, who refused to submit to Russian dominance and pay fur tax, or *yasak*. In fact, Yuri Slezkine, an American historian specializing in Russia, has estimated that 6 percent of all Yukaghir men served as auxiliary soldiers in the part of the Cossack regiment that operated in northeastern Siberia between the 1670s and 1780s.[1] However, the Chukchi were not easily subdued. Russia waged a brutal war against them that lasted three years, from 1744 to 1747.

The campaign was led by Major Dmitry Pavlutsky, who was ordered to expel the Chukchi from their homeland on the tundra and move them by force to the southern areas of Yakutia.[2] At this point, the Chukchi's only weapons were made of stone and bone, and it was regarded as a minor matter to defeat a small group of "primitives." And indeed, Pavlutsky charged brutally forth and quickly became a notorious and hated figure among the Chukchi. In their storytelling tradition, his face is described as covered in a beard as stiff as the whiskers on a walrus, and his sword so broad that it shaded the sun. His eyes were of iron, round and black, and he wore armor so that no arrow could kill him.[3] When he attacked a camp with his Cossacks and Yukaghir hirelings, prisoners were never taken. Everybody was killed: men, women, and children. The people fled in all directions, but they were always found by the army and killed, or else they committed mass suicide to avoid falling into the hands of the Cossacks.

Pavlutsky's luck did not turn until March 14, 1747. He attacked a Chukchi camp with his army of ninety-seven Cossacks and thirty-five Yukaghirs. But the Chukchi had organized a crafty ambush, and soon the notorious fighter and his men were surrounded by six hundred warriors. By nightfall, all his soldiers had been killed. Pavlutsky himself was taken prisoner. The hatred of him was so great that he was roasted on the fire and cut into small pieces, and his flesh thrown to the dogs. It is said that his head was kept as a trophy among the Chukchi for several generations afterwards.[4] Pavlutsky's military expedition became the last that Russia organized against the Chukchi. From the pinnacles of power in the Kremlin came the decision to give up further confrontation and let the Chukchi live according to their own laws—a resolution that extraordinarily lasted until the Communist takeover. It simply cost more than it yielded to subjugate them. An anemic decree confirmed that the Chukchi had been only partially conquered by the Russian Empire and were due to pay tribute to the extent they themselves wished to do so.[5]

As a result of their alliance with the Russians in the war against the Chukchi, the Yukaghirs were given special status as the central power's indigenous soldiers, who staked their lives for the state in the confrontation with Russia's enemies. In terms of local politics, this meant first and foremost that the Chukchi for decades afterwards attacked the Chuvantzi, who are the group of Yukaghirs living closest to the Chukchi. Most of the Chuvantzi were killed, and the few who survived fled to Russian settlements, where they assimilated into the local Cossack community.[6] Nevertheless, the Yukaghirs' special relationship to the Kremlin as the direct protector of the people was cemented, and this would turn out to have extraordinarily great significance in future centuries.

During the terrible famine of 1897, when a large part of the population of Kolyma died, the czar organized emergency aid for the Yukaghirs, bypassing the local administration in Yakutsk, who were observing the famine passively. The special relationship to the central power also continued under Communism. The Yukaghirs were presented as a textbook example of an oppressed group that for centuries had been subdued by their strong, class-conscious neighbors, the Sakha and Chukchi.[7] They were awarded status as a primitive Communist people, an oppressed but collectively orientated minority, with no concept of private property.

As a result, the Kremlin generously sent an apparently endless stream of resources to Nelemnoye. As one of my friends in Yakutsk, who worked as a schoolteacher in the village in the 1980s, told me, "In Nelemnoye you could buy everything that was unavailable in other Siberian towns: Moldavian wine, coffee, chocolate, and sausages. If anything was missing in the local store, it only took a phone call, and a helicopter was immediately sent off with new supplies."

For the Yukaghirs, who had been driven to the edge of the abyss in the period up to the Russian Revolution, Soviet rule involved great material advantages. But there was also a price to pay: several Yukaghir hunters participated in the Stalin administration's manhunt. When prisoners escaped from the barbed-wire fences of the Gulag camps and disappeared out into the taiga, the hunters were sent off to track them down. If they came back with the bodies of the escapees, each of them was given two bottles of vodka and a pair of Russian felt boots (Russian, *valenki*). I have seen old Yukaghir men weep as they confessed their sins as "Stalin's bloodhounds." But back in the 1930s and 1940s, they were considered true patriots, who combated Russia's enemies as their ancestors had previously combated the Chukchi.

The Yukaghirs have without doubt earned significant state care as a result of their special status as the central power's assistants. In 1957, when the Soviet Union conducted a comprehensive political reform that converted the small collective farms in Siberia into large state farms, the local administration in Zyryanka wanted to abolish Nelemnoye and move the population by force to Zyryanka. But the Yukaghirs in Nelemnoye assembled in protest and wrote to the Kremlin to express their dissatisfaction. Shortly afterwards, a decree came from Premier Khrushchev in which the local authorities were ordered to abandon their plans. The official line was that it would be in conflict with the principles of Soviet nationality policy, by which the Yukaghirs as a particularly vulnerable minority were to be protected from assault by the neighboring peoples.

The Crisis Is Resolved

In brief, as Russia's allies, the Yukaghirs have a long tradition of being specially favored by the powers that be in the Kremlin, and Shadrin attempts to invoke this state favor by writing directly to President Putin's administration for help.

And indeed, it turns out that Shadrin's distress call is in fact heard in the Kremlin. He continues his account:

"A few weeks after the letter had been sent, my mother called me to tell me that the president of Yakutia, Nikolayev, had rung in person and asked to speak to me. As I was not there, he asked my mother to tell me to meet him at his office on that Friday. When I arrived, he was sitting at the end of his gold-adorned desk, and I was shown to a sofa in the room. Petrov was already sitting there. He didn't even glance at me.

"Nikolayev was not exactly in a good mood. In fact, he was furious. He started with a long monologue, in which he chastised Petrov and me in turn for bringing Yakutia into this embarrassing situation where the president of Russia had ordered him to resolve what he described as an ethnic conflict between Sakha and Yukaghirs. 'There is no such conflict,' Nikolayev insisted. 'But now Putin thinks there is, and that's a problem.'

"You see," Shadrin adds, "the relationship between Russia and Yakutia is conflict-ridden. Up through the 1980s and 1990s, there has regularly been ethnic unrest in Yakutsk. Members of the organization Sakha Omuk ["The Sakha People"] are attempting to drive out the Russian immigrants and migrant workers, whom they associate with the detested, centralized system of exploitation.

"President Nikolayev has had some success in containing further conflict. He has made his presence felt in the struggle for increased autonomy for Yakutia, but at the same time has emphasized that the republic needs close collaboration with Russia. This is partly due to the fact that Yakutia, as an Arctic area, is situated at the periphery of the world, with poor infrastructure and low urbanization, but most of all because Yakutia possesses some of the richest raw material reserves in the Russian Federation, and so the central power in Moscow will never permit a fully independent Yakutia.

"It is particularly the diamond industry that is at stake. Yakutia is, second to South Africa, the largest producer of diamonds in the world. In addition, Yakutia possesseses significant reserves of gold, silver, tin, lead, iron, coal, and natural gas. And then of course there is also fur production. These are all natural resources that Russia will not just give up.

"In his election campaign, Putin promised that he would concentrate power in the Kremlin again and make a stand against the influence of local leaders. Putin's administration has most likely used our fur project as an excuse to give the president of Yakutia a political reprimand. This also gave him an opportunity to emphasize that Yakutia is subordinate to Russia. That's why Nikolayev was so angry.

"I hoped that, because of the humiliation, Nikolayev would force Sakhabult to give up its monopoly, which breaches Russian antimonopoly legislation, after all. But that was not the case—on the contrary. Nikolayev looked me sternly in the eyes and said that Sakhabult's monopoly on the republic's fur trade would under no circumstances be abolished and that the Yukaghirs' *obshchina* should sell their furs to them."

Shadrin sighs deeply before continuing: "I at once became downhearted and had almost abandoned all hope of concessions when Nikolayev turned to Petrov and asked him whether it was really true that Sakhabult's compensation to hunters for their furs was so much lower than what they were getting for the furs at the auctions. Petrov tried to reply, but Nikolayev interrupted him with another question, namely, whether it was true that Sakhabult was not supplying the hunters with gasoline, spare parts, and ammunition.

"Petrov was eventually allowed to speak and reluctantly admitted that the situation was something along those lines. 'That will have to change!' Nikolayev thundered. In future, Sakhabult should not take more than 5 to 10 percent in commission for handling the sable furs on the international market. The rest of the money was to go to the hunters. Furthermore, Sakhabult would ensure that the hunters had gasoline, ammunition, and other necessities in the future.

"Nikolayev concluded with a grave admonition to Petrov: 'Sakhabult is a state corporation, not a private enterprise, so you have a moral obligation to think of the well-being of the hunters.' Petrov looked down at the floor in shame. To me he said that the problems had now been solved and he expected that I would not take the matter further with Moscow. Then both Petrov and I signed a contract that Sakhabult should only take 10 percent on our furs but at the same time be responsible for conveying the furs to the international market. When I left the presidential palace, I was thoroughly satisfied."

"But what about our fur project?" I almost scream. "And what about Uffe, will he get his money back?"

I am not as pleased with the agreement with Sakhabult as Shadrin.

In fact, I think that he has betrayed our cause. The Yukaghirs may well get a higher price for their furs, but they will still not get to control the fur trade, and that was the very core of our project.

Shadrin, reading the disappointment in my face, considers for a moment before answering: "You must understand that this is Russia, Rane. We are just small pawns in a bigger game. If it had not been for the fact that Putin had a political interest in supporting us, I probably wouldn't even be alive today. It's really a stroke of luck that we are sitting here together now and that we're both alive. Just look at Maksimov. He's dead—maybe because he stuck his neck out too far. We could easily have ended up the same way. And despite that, we succeeded in getting an advantageous contract in place. If I had not reached a settlement with Sakhabult, how then would we be able to pay Uffe what we owe him? Now the *obshchina* can pay him back as soon as Sakhabult has sold our furs at the auction in St. Petersburg. Besides, you can now go back to Nelemnoye. The arrest warrant for you has been withdrawn."

■ ■ ■

I feel immediate relief spread through my body. In a way, Shadrin is right. Compared to all the hazards we have been through—he as a hunted outlaw in Yakutsk, and I as a starving refugee in the taiga—maybe the outcome is not so bad after all. I feel a little embarrassed about having attacked him, and send him a shy smile. After all, I should actually be happy. Finally I can go back to Nelemnoye and after that home to Denmark.

I look out the open door of the cabin, out at the ice-cold stillness that has surrounded me for so long. The taiga is, as always, silent, as if it has been listening in on Shadrin's exciting story. Will I ever come back here? Probably not. My woes are fleeting, and my longing for home is greater than everything else. My time in the taiga has undeniably been something of a trial, but now all is well, bright, and warm, in my very soul. I notice that I no longer feel hunted by a constant, exhausting unease.

It turns out, however, that it is too soon to celebrate; my problems are not over yet.

The Accident

Old people who have personal experience of living under harsh conditions are noted for having a quite special relationship to food: they simply cannot bring themselves to throw it away. Even if it is rotten or otherwise spoilt, they feel an obligation to consume it. Everything edible, regardless of its condition, is sacred for them.

So it is for old Spiridon. He was often hungry as a child. When times were really bad, the family ate all their reindeer-skin clothing, which were cut into thin strips and boiled. Only his father's clothes were untouched. After all, he had to go out in the winter taiga to look for game. The rest of the family sat naked back in the tent. When the children went out to pee, they had to stamp around in the ashes from the fire to try to keep their feet warm in the snow.

But Spiridon's attachment to spoilt old food turns out to be fatal. The day before our departure for Nelemnoye, he eats a lump of rancid butter that has been lying fermenting over the summer, and develops severe stomach cramps. During the night, his temperature rises to boiling point, and he begins to vomit blood.

All four of us stand desperately watching his death struggle. Half unconscious, he yells, "Get lost, you bitch! Let me be!" It is Spiridon's helper spirit, the owner of the River Omulevka, who is trying to kill him.

"She loves Dad and so gives him moose time after time. But she is a cunning demon. Now she's trying to kill him so she can live with him in the Land of Shadows," Yura explains to me.

Suddenly Peter comes in dragging Bim, Spiridon's old hunting dog, who is whining and snapping out at him in terror. Peter draws his long hunting knife and gets ready to stab the dog in the heart, when Spiridon shouts from his bunk, "Let the dog be, you idiot! I'll survive."

Peter was going to sacrifice Bim in the hope that the owner of the Omulevka would accept the dog's soul instead of Spiridon's. Bim and Spiridon have lived together for so long that they have almost grown into each other. And Spiridon will not give up his best hunting dog, who is also his closest friend, even if it might save his life.

All night he lies helpless on his bunk, screaming. This loner, who has not yet given up the Yukaghirs' old way of thinking, is the last master hunter in Nelemnoye. If he dies, many people in the village will end up without meat.

• • •

In the morning, we get ready to leave. Spiridon is wrapped in furs and laid on Sinitskiy's sled, because his snowmobile is the fastest. The sleds on the other two snowmobiles are loaded with meat; they look almost like mobile abattoirs. As for me, I sit on top of the meat, with Peter. The taiga is bathed in orange spring sunlight; its golden rays cast a soft shine on the larch trees, which stand waving their millions of buds in joyful, wild unrest and desire for change. Spring in Siberia is a hot blaze of warmth and light, which hectically breathes life into all the colors of the sky and all the shades of the forest. The air literally buzzes with cheerful, joyful twittering.

Like everything in the taiga, the spring concert is simple and straightforward but yet impossible to represent in notes and difficult to describe in words. The energetic whistling of the small birds, the sorrowful screeches of the cranes, and the crazy squealing of the Arctic loons are gripping, full of poetry, and awaken joy in me—joy at life's vigorous waking up after the long, dark winter. This is what the forest must have looked like for the primeval hunter as he liberated himself from his stinking winter cave and stepped out into the open, restless landscape.

But one must not be seduced by the lavish beauty and life force of spring. It is a time that is in many ways more difficult and deadly than the winter. Small brooks of crystal-clear meltwater flow everywhere. Even though it is still damned cold, the snow is thawing before our eyes, and when the meltwater collects on top of the permafrost, the forest floor is turned into a gigantic puddle. The snowmobiles constantly get stuck in the wet snow, and the rivers, where the ice is about to break away, are a real nightmare to cross.

There is a loud crack and a howl. It is Peter, crashing through the ice. He flails around desperately and repeatedly tries to drag himself up out of the hole, but each time he slides helplessly back into the ice-cold water. Yura lies on his belly, crawls over to Peter, and passes his rifle butt to him. Peter takes hold of the wooden stock, and after a few attempts, Yura succeeds in pulling him up. It is impossible to get the clothes off him. Everything is frozen together in an armor of ice. Yura takes his hunting dagger and slashes the clothes apart. The rest of us pitch the tent and light a fire in the little metal stove. Soon Peter is sitting shaking in front of the roaring stove, filling himself with hot tea. This time it went well, but that is far from always the case. Drowning is one of the commonest causes of death among the Siberian trappers. Each year there are reports of bodies washed ashore, brought down the rivers with the meltwater.

We have lost time, and Spiridon is very poorly. It is decided that Sinitskiy will drive ahead with Spiridon on his sled in the hope of getting him back to the village before it is too late. The rest of us crawl on. Late in the evening, five days after we left Omulevka, something emerges in the evening haze, at first transparent and not quite real, but then gradually more clear. It is the lights of Nelemnoye flickering. I become quite dizzy with delight when Ivan opens the door and embraces me. Spiridon is still alive. We actually made it, we arrived alive. Finally back to civilization.

Now life is to be enjoyed. I can already feel my body screaming for alcohol.

9

THE CURSE

THE DANGER of desperately clinging to one single goal is the disappointment felt once it is achieved. This is how it is with our return to Nelemnoye. For far too long, I have been completely consumed by the desire to escape from the wilderness and get back to the village, back to people and civilization. During meals in the taiga, my longing for the luxury goods of the village—vodka, chocolate, and cookies—became an uncontrollable desire.

When I walked alone in the woods, I fantasized that the larch trees transformed into young village women in elegant leather boots and stylish outfits. During my dreams at night, they came to me undressed. My thoughts were constantly, restlessly driven toward the village. In my head, Nelemnoye has become synonymous with inconceivable pleasure and comfort, which the wretched little village obviously does not live up to in real life. Just the encounter with the dire routines of village life knocks me out completely. Nothing happens, and then even less of the same.

Time evaporates relentlessly in the monotony. Boring, damned boring. Before long I am sleeping most of the days away. At night, I hang out with Peter and some of the other young hunters, eagerly trying to drown their boredom in booze. We are not drinking vodka, but "Royal," 99 percent pure alcohol, which we mix with water. It

PREVIOUS: The main street of Nelemnoye.
FACING: A young Yukaghir woman.

is the cheapest and most common drink in Siberia, an everyman's drink. I have moved into a modest room so that Ivan no longer controls how I spend my days. I do not see much of Yura or Sinitskiy, either. They are busy with their families.

I consider going to Zyryanka and then back to Denmark, but I quickly abandon that plan. At first, I convince myself that I still need to collect ethnographic data, but I soon realize that I am still mentally trapped in the wilderness. The thought of the big city with its crowds of people, sounds, and smells scares me to death. Besides, civilization's values, money, career, and bourgeois marriage have clearly become questionable to me—to such an extent that I have to regularly drink myself out of my senses to repress the gnawing conflict in my mind: Should I go all the way, turn my back on civilization, and settle down permanently as a hunter here among the Yukaghirs?

■ ■ ■

One night, when I am mildly drunk, I let my tongue run away with me, throwing out a snide remark about the Shalugin family: "Kolya and his fat wife have done nothing but try and squeeze money out of me ever since I met them."

Peter and the other hunters laugh loudly. I do not even notice Shalugin's son Maksim, who is standing in a corner and hears everything. Grim-faced, he leaves the room, while I stagger home to my room and climb into my sleeping bag under the stretched-out mosquito net.

During the night, I am woken by the bang of my door being kicked open. I almost automatically raise my hands above my sleeping bag, clenching my fists. A few seconds later, the mosquito net is torn away, and I catch a glimpse of Maksim with a knife in his hand, yelling, "You devil!" He does not manage to say any more before I hammer my fist into his face. He falls over on his back. I jump out of bed, lift him up, and whack him again.

"Have you had enough?" I yell.

He mumbles something incomprehensible, and I smell the alcohol on his breath. I grab his shirt collar, drag him to the door, and fling him out onto the street. Then I slam the door, which can now no longer be locked. I pull out a vodka bottle from under the bed, take a series of big gulps, and lie down again.

After about twenty minutes, Maksim kicks the door in again, this time armed with a shotgun.

When a violent event suddenly occurs while you happen to be quite inebriated, it can be difficult to remember the exact sequence of events, even though each of them stands out quite clearly in your memory. I remember getting out of bed in utter confusion. Maksim raises the gun and aims.

"This is the end," I think, closing my eyes.

At the same instant, the rifle barrel is knocked aside by a hard blow. It is Dusha, who has come to my rescue. She showers Maksim with blows of a broomstick, swearing at him all the while. He falls to the ground and creeps out the door, trying to ward the blows off with his arms. Soon he has vanished. Dusha throws me a mean look and leaves my room in silence. I run over, slam the door, and jam the back of a chair under the doorknob so the door cannot be opened from the outside.

Then I take another series of gulps from the vodka bottle, pull out my hunting dagger, and lie down with the naked blade out.

"If that idiot returns, he'll get a taste of my knife," I mutter, and after a while I doze off.

A Fatal Affair

I stay in bed the whole of the following day. I eat nothing, but only smoke cigarettes and drink vodka, so in the end my head starts spinning and I collapse. I do not wake up until late evening, when somebody knocks on the door.

Still dazed from the booze, I sit up in bed.

"It's only me, open the door." I recognize the voice. It is Rosa, Dusha's younger sister. Her tone is calm and has a melodic rhythm to it, as if she is singing when she speaks. I pull a pair of trousers on, remove the chair, and open the door.

"Are you in bed? Are you sick?"

I do not manage to reply before she slips past me into the room, where she sits down on the bed. A sweet scent of perfume lingers in her wake.

144 • THE CURSE

"What's this I hear, were you about to kill my nephew?" She laughs and signals with her hand for me to sit down on the bed next to her. Which I do.

"You want something to drink?" I ask, my voice hoarse from smoke and alcohol, waving the empty vodka bottle.

"Phew!" she grumbles. "You've turned out like the other hunters, a real boozer." I send her an embarrassed, seasick smile.

She laughs again and places her hand on my thigh. I turn to face her and look into her face. Unlike most women in Nelemnoye, who quickly turn ugly with age, Rosa's face is still beautiful, with silky soft skin, high cheekbones, and delicate slanted eyes. Her smile is blasé, unabashed, and naughty. There is practically no distance between us. I press my lips against hers. Our eyes close, and we fling our arms around each other, while our kisses become more and more uninhibited. They are far too insistent and eager to be called beautiful and delicate.

I am on the verge of brutality when she pushes me away and says breathlessly: "Not like that. It must be gentle."

"Okay," I whisper, and throw her down on the bed anyway.

Practically everything we throw ourselves into passionately is a substitute for something else. That is how it is with Rosa and me, too. I am not in love with her. To me, it is about finding my way back to the female sex and lovemaking after many months of deprivation in the wilderness. Rosa is obviously not in love with me, either. She hardly knows me. But she was crazy about my twin brother and waited in vain for years for him to return to Nelemnoye. And now she has scored his brother, physically a faithful copy of the man she fell in love with. Perhaps it is the fate of an identical twin that a woman wants both once she has fallen in love with one. At least this is what has often happened in my own life—once even giving rise to massive heartache.

But in Rosa's case, there is probably something else going on. She is single, in her midthirties, with no children. In a community like Nelemnoye, that means not just low status but also financial insecurity. Who will take care of her when she is old or sick if she has no children? In other words, she is desperate to find a man to start a family with. I was actually aware of this when I got involved with her.

Maybe it was my own selfish way of testing myself. When it comes to the crunch, am I willing to start a family here in Siberia? The answer is no.

When I wake the next morning, Rosa is gone. I go out in the street, where two men are hanging out.

"Allow me to congratulate you on your forthcoming wedding." The man speaking lifts his cap and bows. The other one watches me with a sour, half-invisible smile.

"What the hell are you on about?" I snap.

"Haven't you heard? Rosa has told the whole village you're getting married." The man bursts out laughing, and the other follows suit. I grumble a couple of swearwords and head for Rosa's apartment. I need to kill that bloody story right away.

When I open the front door and call her name, she comes to meet me with open arms.

"Darling, it's so good to see you. I've missed you so much," she says with a smile.

"What the hell are you going around telling people? Do you think I'm going to marry you just because we've spent one night together?" I throw her a distrustful look.

"Don't worry, my love," she laughs. "We'll be happy once we get to know each other." She embraces me and starts kissing my face. I feel like I am going to choke.

"Leave me alone. It's over!" I yell, pushing her away from me.

At first, she just gapes at me, as if she has not understood what I have just said. Then her face contorts in anger. Her eyes contract into narrow slits and her lips tremble. She rushes to the woodpile in the kitchen, grabs a large stick, and lashes out at me. I try to ward her off with my arms, but her blows hit me on the side of my head, sending blood gushing from my nose. I jump two steps back and am about to yell something when she gives me another blow.

"You bloody bastard! You're even worse than your fucking brother!"

She raises the stick for another blow while I run backwards toward the front door, where I trip over the doorsill and out onto the steps. A neighbor opens his door. He watches me curiously but does not intervene. Rosa stands in her doorway, threatening me with the stick. She mutters a cryptic formula in Sakha that I do not understand, and then spits ritually in the air.

Then she screams in Russian, "Now, nothing will succeed for you! Just wait and see!" She turns around and slams the door behind her.

I get up and blow the blood out of my nose. Then I look at the neighbor, an elderly man, and ask him what she muttered.

"It was a curse," he says. "Bad luck now hangs over your head." Then he, too, slams the door in my face, as if to ward off misfortunes.

Not even a month has passed since I escaped the troubles of the wilderness and returned to Nelemnoye, and I am already up to my neck in problems. Kolya Shalugin and his wife, Dusha, despise me. Their son Maksim has tried to kill me twice, and Dusha's youngest sister, Rosa, has thrashed me with a piece of firewood and cast a curse on me.

Village life has become too unpleasant for me to stay. I again consider whether it is time to go home to Denmark. But I do not feel ready. Instead, I must go back to the taiga.

The Power of the Curse

I find rescue in an elderly Yukaghir couple, Akulina and Gregory. Akulina is the "grandmother" who sewed all my winter clothes from reindeer skin, and Gregory made the moose skin–covered skis I used during my winter hunts. To thank them, I gave them most of the moose meat I brought home from the taiga—nearly half a ton. That was the beginning of a close friendship with the two old people.

Gregory is deaf and has been since his youth. This makes him completely dependent on Akulina, who functions not only as his interpreter but also as his hunting partner. She is his ears, so to speak, and shows him the direction when the dogs bark. But Gregory is always the one to kill the game, since, as Akulina says, "That's the man's job."

In the course of the fifty-five years that have passed since they got married, the two have become inseparable. Never have I seen a couple show such devotion to each other. Akulina's eyes gleam almost every time she looks over at Gregory, and when she looks away during meals, he puts the best, most tender pieces of meat on her plate—despite the fact that he is the one with no teeth.

I tell Akulina about my unfortunate incident with Rosa, but I do not mention anything about the curse. Akulina looks at me with strong, good eyes, as a grandmother looks at a grandchild who has misbehaved, and says authoritatively, "You must learn to stay away from unmarried women of a mature age. They're utterly unreliable."

She asks me if I want to go out with Gregory and her to their hunting cabin some distance up the Yasachnaya River. Yura, who is their close friend, will also be joining them to hunt moose. I do not have a moment of doubt. Get me out of this backwater!

■ ■ ■

The next morning, I walk down to the riverbank, where two aluminum boats are pulled up on the ice by the bank. Gregory and Yura are preparing an outboard motor each, while Akulina is loading cooking equipment, reindeer skins, and other gear into the boats. At the end of May, the river is almost completely open, with occasional ice floes floating by and an ice front that is quickly being eaten away. The landscape is under transformation, too. Only here and there along the bank are there still lumps of old snow. The thaw has turned the ground into a gigantic mud pond, and it squelches with every step. The fur boots have been replaced with high rubber boots.

Before long, we are sitting in the boats, drifting downstream. Yura quickly manages to get his outboard motor going, but Gregory keeps struggling with his. Again and again, he pulls the starter cord. The capricious motor growls a little, then dies out. He pulls out his toolbox, takes the motor apart, and cleans the spark plug. Then he tries again, but the result is the same. The whole thing repeats itself once more, and yet again. But then, "Vroom!" and the boat races upstream. Gregory laughs and waves his hat triumphantly. Akulina grins too, sitting in the open boat, wrapped up in her woolen scarf.

Careening sharply, the two little dinghies swerve in and out of the many crooked curves of the Yasachnaya River. One half-sunken tree trunk or ice floe, and we are done for, but nobody seems to worry about that. We all enjoy the speed spring has brought.

After only two hours' cruise, we reach the cabin. It looks like the ones I have already stayed in, except this one has a plank floor and real glass in its sole window. The place is well chosen: wild and desolate with an extraordinarily good view. Around the cabin, which is situated on a small ridge, a thinly vegetated taiga stretches out: wind-blown, pathetic larch trees in scattered clusters will not prevent us from spotting moose in a half-mile radius of the cabin window.

In front of the cabin, close to the river, stands a tall larch tree. Its trunk is leaning out over the bank and will soon be swallowed by the water. All over its branches hang ribbons, bottles, empty cartridges, and other decorative bits and pieces. When I ask Akulina about the tree, she explains that it is her "double soul." In her youth, before marrying Gregory, she sought the tree in marriage by dancing and singing for it. It gave its consent by gently moving its branches in the wind. Since then, the tree has acted as her "guardian," and it will knowingly take her place whenever she is threatened by some disease. "You see how we have been growing old and weak together," she explains. "Soon the tree will die, and I with it. The two of us are connected, truly."

Among the neighboring Eveny, a population of reindeer herders, we find the same principle of a guardian but in the form of a reindeer, which, according to British anthropologist Piers Vitebsky, stands in for a human during illness but also parallels that human's death.[1] Surely, this willingness to substitute for a human and to die of its own free will in place of the human expresses the deepest sense of the intimacy that binds the indigenous Siberian peoples to their environment. The human and its double are so closely identified with one another that they form two sides of one and the same existence.

We unload while Yura proceeds out into the sparse woods to search for moose. Before long, the stove is crackling. Gregory and I are sitting on narrow benches beside a massive wooden table, eating the fish soup Akulina has brought with her.

Failing Hunting Luck

After dinner, I step out into the cool evening air. I look up at the sky and see the wonder of the northern lights. In a huge, blazing band of whitish yellow, blue, and green colors, the light billows back and forth in every direction. The deep silence is interrupted only by the water lapping at the edge of the ice, which sparkles like a white diamond in the glow of the northern lights.

The Sakha call the northern lights "Yukaghir fires." This may stem from a Yukaghir legend that tells how their people used to be so numerous that the reflections from their many fires created the rolling waves of flame of the northern lights.[2] These days, the Yukaghirs consist of only a small handful of hunters driven to the brink of the precipice. The youngest no longer speak their own language but only Russian. Most of them are alcoholics and die of disease or accidents before they reach the age of fifty. The tide of tuberculosis flows high, and, as for other Arctic peoples, the suicide rate is among the highest in the world.[3]

I recall when during the 1993 expedition I witnessed a Yukaghir mother being told her son had hanged himself in one of the public restrooms in Nelemnoye. She stood stock-still, as if nailed to the ground. Her face turned rock hard and completely expressionless. She displayed neither pain nor grief. Back then, I thought, "The Yukaghirs are used to it—that's why she looks that way."

Only a person who has never known real grief would think that way—that those who suffer are used to it, that they no longer feel the way you do. But no mother can come to terms with the fact that her child has killed himself. She just learns not to express her grief in public.

When I returned to Nelemnoye in 1999, the Yukaghir mother had died. People told me that the grief of losing her son had driven her to the bottle and that she had drunk herself to death. The situation of the Yukaghirs is truly disheartening, and it seems inevitable that, before long, they will fade away completely.

My somber thoughts are interrupted when Yura returns from the hunt. Highly agitated, he steps into the hut.

"I met the Big One. She was only fifteen feet away from me. I shot and shot and emptied the entire magazine. But she just stood there, pulsating like a giant heart, in and out, then turned her back on me and walked away. Not one of my bullets hit her. Something's wrong!" Yura exclaims.

Akulina listens for a while, then nods pensively and begins to enquire whether Yura or his closest family have committed any sinful act, whether they have let the dogs gnaw on the lower leg or head of a moose, or whether they have failed to share their meat with others.

Yura denies that he or his family is guilty of any kind of transgression.

"On the contrary," Yura snaps. "Last night, an old woman visited me in a dream and gave me a piece of bread and butter. The layer of butter was thin, so I asked her to spread it thicker, which she did. I know she gave me good luck for the hunt. But then why this?"

■ ■ ■

The Yukaghir word for "luck" is *pe'jul*, which is also the name for the hunted animal's individual guardian spirit or "owner." The two words are in fact identical.[4] Some hunters describe the *pe'jul* quite physically, as a little bald gnome who can be seen riding on the neck of the moose, while others claim that it lives in the knots of cartilage that are occasionally found on the animal's throat, neck, or shoulders. But even though the Yukaghirs' description of *pe'jul* is tangible, it is still difficult to understand, because luck is both a physical quantity and a kind of "aura" that follows the hunter and that he can maintain or lose, depending on circumstances.

The Yukaghirs have a multitude of ways in which you can lose your *pe'jul*. For instance, if a hunter breaks a taboo, the spirits may punish him by depriving him of his *pe'jul*. You can also inadvertently pass your luck on to other people. This may happen if you lend your rifle or any other hunting tool to a stranger. I remember that I once tried to borrow a pair of skis from a Yukaghir hunter, but he turned me down on the grounds that "he would thereby risk transferring his speed to me."

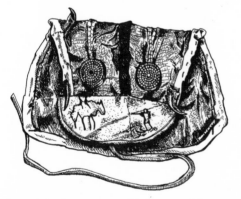

Things are thus also imbued with a sort of luck that may be lost. And then, of course, there are curses, which not only deprive you

Hunter's sewing purse made from swans' feet. The front shows the hunter's encounter with a moose, whose guardian spirit, the *pe'jul*, is riding on its back. Drawing by Marie Carsten Pedersen.

of your luck but may also have an infectious effect, striking everyone among your close family and acquaintances with misfortune.

I listen in silence to the conversation between Yura and Akulina, recalling in terror Rosa's curse. Could this be the reason Yura has lost his hunting luck, and should I tell them about it? When somebody loses his hunting luck, it may take months or even years for it to return, and there is apparently no accepted method to speed up the process. So the situation demands that I lay all my cards on the table.

"Uh, Rosa said some kind of curse over me. She claimed that nothing would work out for me ever again. Could that have something to do with it?" I ask quietly and a little awkwardly.

Yura's face turns bright red. I have never seen him so angry. His eyes flash like lightning, and he stamps his rubber boots on the floor.

"What the hell are you saying, kid? Your affair with that filthy witch has cost me my hunting luck. You idiot!" Yura yells.

Fortunately, Akulina comes to my rescue, interrupting him in an authoritative tone.

"Calm down! The boy didn't know any better." Then she looks over at me.

"Go outside and look to the southwest, toward Nelemnoye, and then say the following: 'Rosa. I'm sorry. I love you. Forgive me.' That's all!" Akulina looks at me insistently.

This has got to be the stupidest thing I have ever heard. The laughter is bubbling right under my larynx. Yura notices and immediately gives me a hissing reprimand. So there is no way around it. I step outside and, closely supervised by Yura and Akulina, repeat her words, one by one. Then I step back in and close the door.

"Now Rosa's poisonous words have been banished," Akulina mutters. "Tomorrow we shall see the result. But you must find a real shaman who can put an end to her curse. Until then, bad luck will cling to you."

Akulina breathes heavily and lies down on the wooden bunk next to Gregory. The rest of us are also exhausted from an atmosphere that is laden with negativity. We follow her example and lie down to rest. The conversation has stopped. Everybody lies there, lost in his own thoughts. Heavily burdened, I implore the spirits that tomorrow may bring something good.

My thoughts drift to accounts of how my predecessor the Russian anthropologist Waldemar Jochelson apparently brought misfortune on the Yukaghirs by attempting to bring a sacred wooden figure back to the American Museum of Natural History in New York.[5] The story goes that in 1878, when a fatal epidemic of smallpox killed off many Yukaghirs, their shamans decided to make a protective offering to the spirit of the disease by carving out of a tree a life-size wooden figure in the image of a young girl—a *chuchelo,* meaning puppet or mannequin in the Russian language. The figure, which was placed opposite the mouth of the Shamanika River, a tributary to the Kolyma River, was quite lifelike, with carved eye sockets and large dark stones for eyes, a costume, and all the features and the appearance of a real young woman. "The aim of this ransom," the Yukaghir writer Teki Odulok wrote, "appeared to be that the spirit of the disease took the figure and gave her own son as a husband for the *chuchelo.* After this, naturally she could not disturb the Yukaghirs any longer because she was at the mercy of her kinsmen."[6]

But then disaster struck: the bride was kidnapped by a foreigner, the former political exile Jochelson, who had close ties to the American Museum of Natural History and its leading anthropologist, Franz Boas. Boas had organized the Jesup North Pacific Expedition to collect art, artifacts, and folkloric texts from the indigenous peoples of northeastern Siberia and the northwest coast of America. Jochelson was hired to lead the Siberian side of the expedition, and his group's accumulation of objects was unprecedented, with over five thousand indigenous items.[7] Jochelson wanted to bring the *chuchelo* to the museum as part of his Siberian collections, but this had terrible consequences. The spirit got angry with the Yukaghirs, its former kinsmen, and took revenge by killing off several clans in Verkhne Kolyma.[8] Perhaps Jochelson himself was also afflicted by the spirit's curse because, although the figure mysteriously disappeared before he reached America, his own life took an unfortunate turn, and he died in poverty as a lonely expatriate in New York.[9]

As I lie mulling over this, I feel that I may have made myself as unpopular with the Yukaghirs and their spirits as Jochelson did in his time. I get hardly any sleep that night.

Luckily, right at daybreak, something fantastic happens. Yura goes out hunting but returns after only an hour. Not only has he shot a moose, the animal walked straight at him. He only had to fire a single shot, and the moose fell at his feet. So Yura seems to have recovered his hunting luck and returns to Nelemnoye with peace of mind. The rest of us have also regained our calm now that the previous day's frustrations have abated.

10

LAND OF SHADOWS

BEING WITH THE OLD YUKAGHIR COUPLE instills a warmth in my heart that I have been missing for too long. I can feel how their affectionate care dispels all my gloomy thoughts. Akulina is constantly laying tidbits on the table in front of me: boiled moose muzzle, raw kidney, and marrow, which I have gradually come to regard as genuine delicacies, but also more conventional treats such as caramels, chocolate, and condensed milk with sugar.

All the while I sit gorging myself, she strokes my hair affectionately, or else she tells one incredible story after the other. Some are ancient myths, while others are her own personal experiences from the taiga, or a mixture of both. They are exciting in any case, and I meticulously write down every single story in the notebook I have brought with me.

In the evening, when I am lying in my sleeping bag, Akulina gives me a goodnight kiss on the forehead, and by day Gregory lends me his SKS automatic rifle so that I can go hunting. With time they even begin to call me their "son," and I have come to love them with the affection of a son.

One evening, when we are sitting chatting, the conversation turns to shamanism. Akulina tells me that even though she knows that there used to be shamans living in Nelemnoye, she never saw them perform. Gregory says nothing, and soon the topic of our conversation changes.

The next morning I go out hunting, and then something strange

Igor Khan, the oldest living Yukaghir.

happens. A bush moves, and a moment later an enormous dark brown bear's head sticks forth, and two peculiar-looking eyes rest inquisitively on me. I give out a small roar but otherwise stand stock-still with my finger ready on the trigger. My heart beats as if my chest is about to explode. Only fifteen feet separates us, and we stand looking at each other without moving. This lasts a minute or two, I suppose, but it feels like a very long time.

Fearful thoughts shoot through my head: "If the bear has cubs nearby, it is sure to hurl itself at me. Should I shoot now, or wait and see?"

I choose to stay calm. The bear turns around, and I feel a twitch, a fine shock through my nerves. I see its hairy shoulder turning, and its shaggy back follows behind, before it finally disappears into the brush. This is like a nod to me. I sense this fine gesture of peace in my blood, and I back slowly away along the path I came.

■　■　■

Safely home in the cabin, I sit down at the table and am about to recount my adventure when Akulina intercepts me. In the course of the day, she has persuaded Gregory to tell me about his mother, who was in fact a shaman (Yukaghir, *a'lma*).

"He has never told it to anybody before, not even me," she explains, "because it was not always easy and actually had a price for his family. But he wants you to know it, because you are our son and he knows that that kind of information is important for your work." Gregory begins to explain in Yukaghir, and Akulina translates into Russian.

"When I was a boy, the men's hunting luck sometimes ran out, and we were left without food. Then my father used to ask my mother for help. 'Do you want me to sin again?' she replied. She was afraid to use her magic powers and only did it when we were starving. The whole family gathered in one room. A willow twig with four branches was placed in the middle of the floor. Then my mother went down on all fours and began to imitate the movements of a moose. A little infant was placed on her neck to represent *pe'jul*. After a while, she fell into a kind of 'trance' (Russian, *kamlaniye*) and began to grunt as she swung her head back and forth like a moose. She then moved over to the twig and began to eat off its branches.

"At that point my father gave me a small toy bow and arrow, and said, 'You see the moose, shoot it in the heart.' This I did, after which my mother fell over on her side, kicking her legs like a dying moose. After that, my father helped my mother over to the bed. She was exhausted. The only thing she said was that the hunters should go out to a certain place in the forest where there was a willow bush with four branches. There she had 'tied' (Russian, *privyazat*) the moose. She said that they should shoot it in the heart so that it would not suffer. They succeeded every time. The men always came back with meat. However, my mother never ate it, saying that she would die if she did. Several others were also afraid and preferred to go hungry.

"When a hunter succeeds in shooting a moose, it is because the animal has given itself to him. Its owner has sent it to the hunter as a gift. So it is the spirit and not the hunter who permits the killing to take place. The shaman, on the other hand, takes the animal by force. She uses her magic powers to tie the animal to a tree against the spirit's will. That makes her extremely vulnerable to revenge attacks by the spirit, who has deliberately withheld the animal from the humans because they have somehow done something wrong. Those who choose to eat the meat may become victims of the animal spirit's revenge.

"For some, the fear is so great that they choose to let the meat lie. However, it is the shaman's own family who run the greatest risk. My mother had twelve siblings, and they all died young. I myself had four brothers and sisters, and there are only two of us left. Akulina and I have managed to have only one child, who is mentally disabled. He can't hunt but always sits at home in the village. We have all paid for my mother's sins."

Today the shamans have disappeared from Siberia. The Soviet anthropologists explain it by saying that shamanism was driven out and neutralized by Communism—how it happened, we are not told—and that the Yukaghir people have finally been liberated from religious superstitions that formerly enslaved them.[1] Now they live in nice wooden Russian houses and are subjected to hygiene inspections. In the same jargon, it is also mentioned that they today use soap and underwear.[2] But does that mean, as the Soviet anthropologists so stubbornly assert, that shamanism has disappeared?

The term *shaman* has become immensely widespread within both anthropology and religious studies.[3] But how are we to understand the word, which is thought to have its origins in Siberia, but today is used much more widely to designate persons within tribal societies who otherwise went by names such as "medicine men," "witchdoctors," "wizards," or "magicians"? In the classical literature about shamanism, the shamans are regarded as constituting a kind of early form of priesthood. The renowned historian of religion Mircea Eliade described the shamans as a "religious elite."[4] The Soviet anthropologists also regarded the shaman as an early form of priest. They asserted that the emergence of shamanism was part of the historical development in which the primitive communistic society was suppressed and replaced by more hierarchical types of society.[5] This linking of shamanism with abuse and exploitation undoubtedly played a part in legitimizing the Soviet regime's antireligious campaign, which led to the killing of hundreds of shamans in Siberia in the 1930s and 1940s.[6]

But does the shaman really belong to a special religious elite, distinguished from others in the society? Not among the Yukaghirs. In fact there is a striking similarity between Gregory's mother's shamanistic behavior and old Spiridon's imitation of the moose during the hunt. In both cases, they gain control over their prey by transforming themselves in its image. The difference between Gregory's mother and Spiridon rests solely in how great a transformation each of them undergoes. The hunter does not become the animal in any absolute sense but moves between animal and human identities. This may cause qualms of conscience in the hunter, who comes to perceive his prey as a kind of person with its own will, thoughts, and emotions. Many Yukaghir myths describe the moral dilemma of living by killing animals, which in reality are humans in disguise. But for the shaman, this feeling of anxiety at killing and eating the animal is even stronger than for the hunter, because during the trance she becomes one with the moose. She cannot eat the animal's flesh, as that would involve dabbling in cannibalism or even a kind of auto-cannibalism. She has to forgo the meat.

Clearly, the shaman's world is not categorically different from the hunter's, and her actions and experiences are a specialized or intensified form of those of the hunter. Shamanism among the Yukaghirs has nothing to do with a religious elite or priesthood but is a much broader phenomenon that is practiced in different ways by completely ordinary hunters. So we cannot say that shamanism in Siberia has disappeared, just because there are no longer any shamans. Instead there exists a broad and all-pervading form of everyday shamanism, which is put into practice through the hunters' sexual dreams of spirits and their imitation of the moose during the hunt, among other things. This kind of "do-it-yourself" shamanism survived Communism's campaigns of terror and is a living part of the contemporary Yukaghirs' life.[7]

■ ■ ■

After a good month together, the old couple and I head home to Nelemnoye. In the dusk during the boat trip, we hear an owl whose hooting sounds like a soul plaintively requesting permission to depart: an ill omen of a recent death that holds true. It is old Spiridon who is dead. This loner who could not stand the fixed rhythms of settled life had been chained to the bed by illness. In a last desperate attempt to regain his freedom, he had gotten up but had fainted after a few paces and broken his neck in the fall.

In accordance with Russian Orthodox tradition, he now lies in an open coffin on show for relatives and friends. When my own father died, I saw his rigid, uninhabited body lying on the bed at home, but Spiridon's body is different. It seems to be engrossed in action, as if he is really doing what he always claimed to be able to do in dreams: voyaging in the spirit world. At the moment of death I suppose he had made the dream into reality.

The Other Moscow

The day after the funeral, I go to visit Nikolay Likhachev, or Igor Khan as he is called in the village. Apart from a Christian name, every Yukaghir also has a nickname, which has the purpose of confusing the evil spirits. The nickname may be in Yukaghir, like Shalugin's nickname, "Choo-Choo," or in Russian such as "Chemodanchik," which means "the Little Suitcase." What the nicknames have in common is their reference to an unflattering trait of the person. Thus, Chemodanchik is a short, fat man with a rather square body build. As for the nickname Igor Khan, nobody can remember the exact meaning anymore. Some think it means "the One-Eyed," because he is blind in one eye.

Igor Khan is special in more ways than one. He is the oldest living Yukaghir. In fact, nobody knows for sure how old he is, not even himself, because he was born before the community registered births. But people estimate that he is at least ninety. His grandfather was one of the last Yukaghir shamans. Igor Khan began the long training to become a shaman himself, but his course was halted by the advance of Communism in the 1930s. Nevertheless, his partial training has given him a special insight into the spirit world. He knows more about the spirits than most and is much more explicit about what he knows. Perhaps for that reason, Igor Khan is a marginalized and feared figure in Nelemnoye. His name is associated with dozens of frightening and inexplicable events. For example, some years ago, he was lying mortally debilitated by tuberculosis. During the night, the dogs of the village began to howl plaintively in chorus, a sure sign that somebody would die. Everybody presumed that it was old Igor Khan who was about to expire. Instead, a youth of only seventeen hanged himself. The next day, Igor Khan was on his feet, running around as if he had been born anew. All traces of tuberculosis had vanished. People in the village claimed he used his magical abilities to steal the boy's good health. So they have warned me against visiting him. But, for me, Igor Khan is a key person in my anthropological fieldwork about the Yukaghirs' belief in spirits, or what anthropologists call "animism."

There is not much anthropological literature on the Yukaghirs to refer to. The last serious ethnography of the Yukaghirs is more than one hundred years old. It was conducted by the Russian anthropologist Waldemar Jochelson, who began to study the Yukaghirs because he was exiled to the Kolyma region due to his revolutionary political activities. Later, in 1926, he published his anthropological material in the book *The Yukaghir and the Yukaghirized Tungus*, which is still the most comprehensive and detailed description of the people.[8] During the Soviet period, only a few books were written about the Yukaghirs, all of which are in Russian and are so infected with ideological censorship that the information that is missing often says more than what is included. The Soviet anthropologists' primary task was to place the Yukaghirs in the Marxist chain of stages of socioeconomic development. For this reason, the people's own voices were almost totally omitted, with the exception of some overenthusiastic statements about the blessings of Soviet society. Instead the reader is presented with old anthropological data from Jochelson, which are used as proof of cultural "relics" from the primordial stage of evolution.[9] Quite uninteresting reading.

Igor Khan's sled dogs howl when I approach his little log cabin, which is hidden away on the outskirts of the village. Igor Khan sticks his wrinkled troll face out. His spiky hair with mixed shades of gray sticks out on all sides like a brush. Under the countless creases and convolutions of his face, I can just glimpse his one functioning, but extremely penetrating, eye, which looks inquisitively at me. He is dressed in a padded jacket and canvas trousers. On his feet he has a pair of long leather boots whose shafts reach almost up to his groin.

"Oh, it's you. Come in," he says in broken Russian, revealing his last two teeth, one in the upper jaw and one in the lower. We go inside. The room, which is equipped solely with a wooden bench and a small table, is indistinguishable from a hunting cabin. There are wood shavings and garbage lying everywhere, and the stench is almost unbearable. But Igor Khan does not seem to mind. His little manikin body, which is just under five feet tall, seems wiry and agile for his age. When he strides forward through the filth, it is as if he is dancing lightly over it, almost without his feet touching the floor.

"What do you want?" asks Igor Khan, and he yawns loudly— a signal to me not to stay too long.

"I'd like to hear about death. What happens when you die?" I ask as I sit down.

Igor Khan smacks his lips pensively. When he goes to say something, he breaks out in a vigorous coughing fit, which ends with a decent gob of spit on the floor. But then the words flow.

"When a human, a moose, or other being dies, its soul (Yukaghir, *ayibii*) travels down to the Land of Shadows (Yukaghir, *Ayibii-lebie*), which is the resting place for all the dead souls. The same applies to a cup that gets broken, or a house that burns down; all their souls travel to the Land of Shadows, where they regain their original shape. The dead souls gather in a colossal city, the *Other Moscow*. I know this because I have been there myself."

I look at him in incomprehension, but Igor Khan continues unabashed.

"Once, when I was hunting, I fell through a hole in the ground. I stood up and looked around me. It was as dark as a tomb. I lit a match and could see footprints leading in through a long passage and on into a cave. I followed the prints and came to a colossal city on the opposite bank of a dark river. Where I was standing, there was a canoe (Russian, *vetka*) with its paddle dripping water, as if somebody had just used it. I sat in the canoe and paddled over to the city.

"It was gigantic. Buildings of all kinds towered up around me: tents, wooden houses, high-rise blocks, and skyscrapers in a total mess. Thousands of people of all nationalities, Yukaghirs, Yakuts, and Russians, were walking around the city. There must have been Danes like you there, too, but at the time I didn't know what they looked like. None of the people could see me. To them, I was invisible.

"I noticed a Yukaghir family living in a bark tent. They were sitting eating rotten meat. It was as black as charcoal. And the tea they were drinking was also completely black. Now I know that it's because they were consuming the "shadows" of our meat and tea. It was disgusting, but I was hungry, so I snatched a piece of meat.

"'Who took my meat?' the daughter cried. But of course none of them could see that it was me. After they had eaten, the family went to bed. I lay down beside the daughter, as used to be the tradition for a guest. She was fat and lovely, so I took my trousers off and penetrated her with my penis.

"The girl gave a terrible howl: 'My tummy hurts! My tummy hurts!'

"Her parents woke up, and when the girl went on screaming, they fetched a shaman.

"I recognized the shaman. It was my grandfather, who had died a few years previously. When he looked at me, it was as if two rays of light went through me: 'You are not dead. What are you doing here?'

"I told him that it was all a mistake and that I just wanted to go home. Then he laid a piece of horse leather in his hand and ordered me to sit on it. In the same instant I was flying through the air on the back of a horse. It went so fast that my ears got cold.

"Suddenly I found myself beside the hole that I had fallen down into. It was morning, and I could see everything clearly. I went home to Nelemnoye. A group of men came and asked me where I had been, as they had been out looking for me.

"'I was in a big city,' I replied.

"'Which one?' they asked. 'There are no big cities here.'

"I asked them how long I had been gone.

"'Two months,' they replied. 'We thought you were dead.'

"I thought I had been gone for only two days. When my father heard about my experiences, he became terror-stricken. 'You've been in the Land of Shadows. We must find that hole and cover it over so that other people don't fall into it.'

"We tried to find the place but couldn't.

"You see, that's why I can tell you for certain where the soul goes after death. When I die, I'll see the lovely girl again."

Igor Khan laughs aloud. I am quite stunned by his account and do not know what to think. I wonder whether he really experienced the realm of the dead, or is the whole thing perhaps something he dreamed? I have already learned that the boundary between dream and reality is fluid and irrelevant in Siberia.

"Does the soul stay living in the Land of Shadows?" I ask.

"No. A person's soul will live in the Land of Shadows until the moment a woman among his or her living relatives becomes pregnant. Then the soul will return to be reborn in the child. The two will then become one and the same person, and the child must be named after the deceased. We always greet a newborn baby with the words: 'Welcome home.'"

A good month after Spiridon's death, one of his grandchildren,

Nadia, gives birth to a little boy. There are great complications at the birth, and Nadia has to be brought by boat to a hospital in Zyryanka. She is not conscious, and people forget all about the infant, who lies practically naked in the boat and nearly freezes to death. In a dream the same night, Yura sees Spiridon standing naked in front of the stove. He is shaking, and his body is completely blue with the cold.

In Zyryanka, the infant is so weakened that the doctors give up trying to save it. But then Yura turns up at the hospital and goes over to the sleeping boy:

"Dad, you've come back. Stay with us," he whispers in the boy's ear. The child opens his eyes and smiles. To the astonishment of the doctors, it regains its vitality and is discharged a week later. The newborn is given the name Spiridon. The Yukaghirs' greatest hunter has come home.

Should We Believe in Reincarnation?

The word *reincarnation* comes from Latin roots, meaning "again-embodiment," which means that the human's soul lives on from life to life in a new physical body. This idea is reflected in the Yukaghirs' own saying about rebirth: *"Shoromo ayibii kel'eil io'nin,"* which means: "A person's shadow (soul) comes back in this person's body."[10] But this is virtually the only thing the Yukaghirs' belief has in common with the more well-known religions from Southeast Asia that believe in reincarnation. For the Yukaghirs, the objective of rebirth is not to get out of the circle of reincarnation, as in the Buddhist or Hindu tradition, where one tries to attain nirvana or *moksha*, the Sanskrit word for "salvation."[11] Instead, the Yukaghirs expect that people must pass through infinite rebirths and bring back character traits that they displayed in their earlier lives. Buddhists and Hindus see reincarnation as dependent on how one behaves in pure moral terms in this world, but I have not found any corresponding idea among the Yukaghirs' beliefs that sinful actions in this life will lead to punishment in the next. A person can indeed be transformed into an evil spirit and get trapped in places where he or she in practice ceases to be active, but there is no fixed idea of "good" and "bad" rebirths. It is not just humans and animals but also objects that are trapped in their own circle of uninterrupted rebirth. In fact it seems as if nothing is excluded from the system and nothing new will be able to enter into it.[12] In principle at least, a fixed number of souls go round and round in an endless cycle.

If a child's identity is not correctly determined and he is given the wrong name, his *ayibii* will be offended and not like him. So it will work against the child rather than helping it in life. For this reason, people in Nelemnoye are very interested in determining their children's true identity. Now and then, a dying person will disclose in advance the woman he or she will attempt to enter. At other times, a woman will dream about a definite deceased person during her pregnancy, and in this way she will know which relative's *ayibii* has returned in her unborn child. In other instances, the child itself will declare who it is when it is two or three years old and has just learned to speak.

For example, a young mother told me that her son was a reincarnation of her great-grandfather, who had died long ago and whom she had not known in person. She discovered this when she once addressed her son by his Christian name, Igor, to which the boy replied, "My name is not Igor, it's Tompúla." The boy was only three years old at that point, and she presumed that he was talking nonsense. Nevertheless, she mentioned the incident to some older relatives, who told her that Tompúla was the nickname of her great-grandfather on her mother's side. This convinced her that her son was in fact a reincarnation of her great-grandfather and that he had been given the wrong name. As a result, now she always calls him Tompúla, even though he was christened Igor. "Since then," she assured me, "my son has become more cheerful and less insolent."

For those of us who adhere to a scientific view of the world, it is difficult to take this kind of story of reincarnation as anything but superstitious beliefs that have nothing to do with reality, because the physical world is all that exists. The soul, or perhaps more correctly the consciousness, is created by the brain, and when it dies, the consciousness dies too. It is difficult to imagine a plausible alternative to this prevalent scientific understanding of life and death. Nevertheless, it is remarkable that around the world we find numerous examples of just precisely what the Yukaghirs describe, namely, children aged two or three who claim to be able to remember events from their previous lives. In certain cases, they provide exceedingly precise details such as names, places, decoration of houses, work, and cause of death—information that the child or its family could not possibly have known.

These cases have led a group of scientists from the University of Virginia, led by the medical doctor and psychologist Ian Stevenson, to research the phenomenon. During the last forty years, he and his group have collated and investigated spontaneous cases of reincarnation around the globe, where children claim to be able to remember details from previous lives. The researchers investigate every case and travel to the place where the child and family live in order to investigate the circumstances closely. They check all of the details provided about the previous life. Today they have about twenty-five hundred reports where they have concluded that the circumstances cannot be explained by any other means but that the child has in fact remembered a previous life.[13] The conclusion is intimidating because it compels us to review our thinking about the very constitution of life. Is it really conceivable that we have lived previous lives? Naturally, Stevenson and his group cannot provide definite proof for the theory of reincarnation, but in purely empirical terms they render the idea probable that the human consciousness can take up residence in a new body, something that science is currently unable to provide a theoretical explanation for.

11

SCREWED

I AM SITTING in Zyryanka's small airport, waiting for the propeller airplane to Yakutsk. A whole year has passed since I returned to Siberia to carry out my field study of the Yukaghirs and revive the fur project. The trip is over; I have finally decided to go home to Denmark. I am neither happy nor sad at the prospect of going home, as I do not know what to expect. Is Helene still waiting for me? Since I last saw her in St. Petersburg, I have received only a few letters, all without much affection. Where am I to live in Cambridge when I am supposed to start writing my PhD thesis about the Yukaghirs' spiritual beliefs? I do not know, and for that matter I am almost indifferent. I feel empty of thoughts and hopes, as if in a meditative state where only the present matters.

I have waited for the airplane for a week, as Zyryanka has been wrapped in a thick fog brought on by the summer heat and the humid climate. Suddenly the fog lifts, and a departure announcement blares over the PA system. As often happens when traveling in Siberia, a long period of waiting is replaced by feverish activity. Quickly, quickly! Those who do not hurry will be left behind without mercy. With hectic motion and loud shouting, suitcases, boxes, and bags are thrown into the airplane's little passenger cabin, and people scramble to sit on narrow benches alongside the mountain of luggage before the rotor blades whine and the plane launches into the air toward Yakutsk.

We immediately lose sight of Zyryanka as white clouds surround the airplane. After twenty minutes pass, the skies clear, and I look

Flying over the Kolyma Upland region of Siberia.

down on the Kolyma Upland's high, sharp slopes and deep river valleys filled with old snow in the ravines. There must be places down
there that no human has ever reached, and who knows, perhaps long-
extinct species of animals still roam there. The indigenous hunters
speak of a gigantic bear—much bigger than an ordinary brown bear,
with very short hind legs and a flat, oblong head—that has been seen
on the outskirts of these mountains. Can it be one of the giants of the
Ice Age, the long-extinct cave bear?

■　■　■

After a six-hour flight, we reach Yakutsk on the bank of the River
Lena, which at 2,750 miles is the tenth longest river in the world. The
Lena rises in southern Siberia, close to Lake Baikal. It flows northeast
onto the Central Siberian Plateau near Yakutsk, where it reaches a
width of up to twelve and a half miles. It forms a vast delta of tributaries, islands, lagoons, swamps, tracts of rushes, and floodplains.

With a population of three hundred thousand, Yakutsk is not just
the capital of Yakutia but the economic and cultural power center
of northeastern Siberia since its founding in 1632. From Yakutsk the
Cossacks embarked on their campaigns of conquest, and from Yakutsk the whole of northeastern Siberia's collection of *yasak* was ad-
ministered. Since the 1950s, the city has had everything that belongs
in a modern urban area: a university, a hospital, government buildings, and hotels. Still, great changes have taken place between my
visits in 1993 and 2000. Beautiful new apartment complexes, shop-
ping malls, and casinos with mirror facades have shot up along the
main streets in the center of the city. There is now an abundance of
food and all sorts of luxuries to buy. The problem is that few people
can afford to take part in the new consumer economy reserved for
the rich. Ordinary wage earners can barely make ends meet by taking two or more jobs.

The liberal reformers claim that this inequality is necessary: the
money and the good things in life function as a carrot for those who
work hard and take advantage of opportunities of the new system.
But so far openness and democratization have mostly just brought
about the legalization of criminality. Those who coldly and cynically

circumvent the law get rich, while those who keep their morals intact and work hard get screwed. In Russia, the market economy means above all extortion, exploitation, and fraud.

Cheated Again

The Yukaghirs' *obshchina* director, Shadrin, is a tragic textbook case of this exploitation. I meet him at my hotel in the center of Yakutsk. He has already been staying for two weeks in the city, where he was to collect the money that Petrov, with President Nikolayev as a witness, had promised him for the confiscated sable furs. But when Shadrin steps into my hotel room, his pale, tired face tells a different story.

"What went wrong?" I ask.

Shadrin shakes his head in resignation.

"You remember how we signed a contract with Sakhabult that they would sell our furs at the fur auction in St. Petersburg for a 10 percent commission?"

"Yes," I reply. "After all, you were almost forced to do so, because Nikolayev wouldn't give up Sakhabult's fur monopoly. But I must say that I never quite understood what you got out of the deal."

"Yes, you do," replies Shadrin, mildly offended. "As you know, the *obshchina's* three hundred sable furs were too few to be sorted in uniform bundles of color shades and quality. That makes the price per fur fall at the auction. The advantage of combining with Sakhabult was that our furs could be bundled together with their many thousand sable furs and we could achieve a higher price per fur. At least, that was the intention. Meanwhile, the bar codes that we marked our furs with and that proved which fur belonged to which hunter were removed by the police on confiscation. I was aware of the problem and told Petrov that he must mark which furs belonged to us before he sold them to the auction. After all, this is what he swore he would do when we met with the president."

"So what's the problem?" I ask.

"The problem arose when I went to Sakhabult's headquarters to fetch the money for our furs after the auction in St. Petersburg. Petrov gave me a printout stating that our furs had been sold for an average price of twelve hundred rubles. That's far less than I expected. As you may remember, we gave each hunter on average an advance of twelve hundred rubles per fur, which was equivalent to about 50 percent of the expected sale price at the auction. We calculated the hunter would get another twelve hundred rubles per fur after the auction. So Petrov now wanted to pay me per fur only what we had already paid out. In addition, Sakhabult wanted a 25 percent commission for having traded our furs at the auction, so we would only get nine hundred rubles per fur."

"Why is that so unjust?" I ask, clearly irritated at what I regard as an expression of Shadrin's sloppiness. "Surely that was in accordance with the agreement you made?"

"Rane, there is a great difference in the price for a single sable fur, depending on grading. The colors alone have eight gradations, and the underwool has four. In addition, the fur is graded according to when in the season it is taken: December and January are the best months; March and April are the worst. Furthermore, defects influence the grading: the fur may be torn or have marks from shots or traps. There may also be bald spots that drag the value down. The very best, black diamond, is a large, blue-black fur with a lot of silver hairs. Without defects, it scores 100 percent, which is the highest grade.

"Out of all the sable furs from Nelemnoye, only 5 percent are graded as black diamonds. Our average fur scores 65 percent, and that's including the very worst pelts. But that's much better than with Sakhabult, where the average fur scores only 52 percent. So I asked Petrov how our sable furs—which are of distinctly better quality than Sakhabult's average fur—only earned an average price of twelve hundred rubles. Petrov replied that our furs had been bundled together with Sakhabult's and that we had received the average price for the total quantity of sable furs that they had sold at the auction."

Shadrin pauses briefly and continues: "I got very angry and asked whether our furs weren't marked so that they could easily be set apart. Petrov just laughed and replied that he knew nothing of that, and that all the furs had been bundled into packs of one hundred or two hundred and sold together. I told him our furs were of a higher quality than the average and demanded that they give us more than the nine hundred rubles per fur.

"Petrov got mad and replied that if I was dissatisfied, he could easily raise the expenses further, and then we would get an even smaller sum per fur. He claimed to be able to do that because Sakhabult had in fact only sold 40 to 60 percent of the total of ten thousand furs that they had submitted to the auction. The unsalable furs would drag the average price down further. So if I wasn't satisfied, he would gladly factor the expenses for these leftover skins into our payment. I realized that I had no choice but to accept the average price of nine hundred rubles per fur."

"So you got screwed!" I say in resignation.

"Yes, you could well say that," replies Shadrin.

"Presumably you can go back to Nikolayev and complain," I insist.

"No. I can't go running to the president every single time I have a problem," replies Shadrin. "The president has spoken and issued his orders. Now his door is no longer open to me. In addition, I can't prove that our furs were of better quality than the average for Sakhabult, because the bar codes have been removed. My word would not be enough."

"Then you must go to the newspapers to let Nikolayev know what has happened and put pressure on Sakhabult," I say. "You can't just ignore Petrov's dirty tricks. Besides, Uffe's loan to the *obshchina* must be repaid. God knows how he will explain this story to his investor."

"Uffe will get his money—at least, most of it," replies Shadrin. "I have already been to the bank and transferred a good six thousand dollars. But there is nothing else we can do now. Nikolayev made it plain during our meeting that he would not tolerate any more public scandal on our part."

Forever Subjugated

For the first time during my stay among the Yukaghirs, I realize that it makes no difference who rules over them: whether an autocratic czar, a Communist dictator, or a democratically elected president, they will always fear him. Like a poison, generations of oppression and terror have circulated fear in the Yukaghirs' blood vessels, infecting every cell. If the ruler disappeared one day, would they then seek a new one? Have they become so dependent on fear that they can no longer live without it? I become totally disheartened and cannot help feeling contempt for Shadrin's cowardice. He probably notices it, because we part in silence, without the usual warmth.

The next day, I take the bus to a dilapidated office on the outskirts of Yakutsk. It belongs to the editorial board of the small local newspaper *Ilken*, which has specialized in writing about indigenous people's affairs. I meet two young journalists, Olga Ulturgasheva and Varvara Danilova, who grew up in the taiga but have spent most of their adult lives in Yakutsk. I tell them my dramatic story: about the Danish–Yukaghir Fur Project, about Shadrin's arrest, about the confiscation of the hunters' sable furs, about Maksimov's mysterious death, and about my life as a refugee in the taiga. They sit wide-eyed, listening intently, and remain silent for several minutes after I have finished my account.

Then Varvara shouts almost triumphantly: "This is bloody different from the local parties and concerts this newspaper normally covers. It will be the article of a lifetime!"

Olga is more reserved, pointing out that it could be dangerous to get into conflict with Petrov and Sakhabult.

■ ■ ■

We end up writing two articles, which are published in the paper a week apart. The first is fairly harmless, as it just reports about the idea behind the fur project.[1] The second article is long and more controversial, accusing Sakhabult of cheating the Yukaghir hunters out of their money and indirectly exhorting the authorities to more closely investigate Maksimov's death, though without accusing Sakhabult of being responsible.[2] I am named as the writer of the first article, but the two journalists decide that it would be too risky to put my name on the second. Accordingly, it is published under "Igor Kolomets," a nickname the hunters had given me.

We nervously await the reaction to the articles. Day in and day out, we sit glued to the telephone, expecting Petrov or some official from the president's administration to ring and comment on the articles. But we do not hear a sound. Not even Shadrin contacts us. Are they totally indifferent, or are they trying to kill the story with silence?

Then suddenly something happens, quite different from what we expected: Sakhabult makes a public announcement that it will raise the payment for the hunters' sable furs by 10 percent. Their reason is that international prices for furs have gone through the roof and indigenous hunters should also benefit from the increased demand. Is Sakhabult's sudden generosity toward the hunters a pragmatic reaction to our articles? Has Nikolayev yet again pushed Petrov to make concessions so as to avoid public scandal? I never get the answer.

The New Russia

Meanwhile, I am involved in a bleak incident at my hotel. I am standing in the corridor, smoking a cigarette out the open window, when a drunken Russian, a man in his fifties, staggers up beside me. I recognize him. He lives three doors down the hall.

"Come and drink with me, comrade [Russian, *tovarishch*]!" he shouts. "Mother Russia is going to ruin, and we are going to ruin with her!"

I turn to face him forbearingly and say, "No, thanks." But he does not intend to let me be.

"Foreigner! Enemy of Russia!" he screams, clenching his fists in anger.

I turn my back to him and begin to walk toward my room when he catches up with me. He brandishes a long-bladed knife and lays the edge against my throat. Struck with terror, I pull my neck away from this uncontrollable madman. He stands shouting after me as I slide in through the door of my room and quickly close it. Back in safety, I sit for a moment on the bed while the blood pumps through my heart like drumrolls. Then I grab the telephone and ring the hotel reception to report the incident.

A half hour later, I hear boots tramping along the corridor. I stick my head out and see a pack of uniformed police officers dragging the man away in handcuffs. He is bawling like a little child, apologizing incessantly, and asking them to let him go. But it makes no difference. The police officers grab his arms, and they disappear together down the stairs. It hurts to see a human being lose his dignity like that, even though his actions against me deserved consequences.

In Siberia, outside the cities, there is space. There are fishing waters and forests where you can hunt and gather berries. Out there, a good man still has an opportunity to get by. The anger and powerlessness are found in the cities, where people feel downtrodden by economic crisis and the uselessness of the new system.

Try to imagine that you have been a loyal citizen. You have sat on the local party board and looked after your public job with care, even with enthusiasm. In your free time, you have devoted yourself to edifying influences such as the pioneer corps. How would it feel then to be told that everything you have devoted your time to, everything you have spent your life on, has been part of the oppression of a reactionary system? This is how it is for the many Russians who believed fully and firmly in Soviet Communism's means and ends and now see the foundations of their existence ripped out from under them. They have only the vodka bottle to relieve the pain and the humiliation. Of course I do not know whether the drunken man is suffering such a fate, but I think he is.

■ ■ ■

The next day, when I stand in front of the hotel and hail a taxi to the airport, I feel frustrated. I thought I could alter the course of three hundred years' brutal exploitation of Siberia's indigenous hunters and help them control trade in their own furs for the first time. The result, after great suffering, privation, and audacity, is insignificant: a minimal price increase for the hunters' furs, for as long as it lasts. Sakhabult has not only maintained its fur monopoly, they have had it cemented by the president of Yakutia himself. The indigenous hunters, on the other hand, are indentured to the superrich parasites and mafiosi of the new Russia.

I open the door to the taxi and stick my head in: "What does it cost to drive to Yakutsk airport?"

"One thousand rubles," the driver replies, staring straight ahead.

I offer him five hundred rubles, but he just shakes his head. I let the idiot drive on and hail another car in to the curb. He also demands a thousand rubles.

"You must be insane!" I scream. "It's only twenty minutes' bloody drive to the airport!"

He laughs and shrugs his shoulders. I am seized with rage. This is the thanks I get for leaving the comfort and security of Denmark to confront Russia's criminals and profiteers. Petty crooks who demand a thousand rubles for a taxi ride are no better than the affluent jackals and parasites, whom I can only regard with a feeling of shame on behalf of humanity. But the driver does not care. He has got me and he knows it. I cannot carry my backpack weighing 150 pounds all the way to the airport. I have to swallow the bitter pill, jump into the car, and pay.

■ ■ ■

I feel like a victim of reason. I came to Siberia to help some of the most deprived people in Russia, the Siberian trappers, and was convinced that by acting on the basis of well-considered plans, I would achieve the right results in the end.

Because this is how I was brought up: No matter how different we humans are, no matter how dissimilar our cultural backgrounds might be, we are all equal by virtue of our reason. If an appeal is made to reason, good will always triumph. But that is not how it has gone— on the contrary. The Kierkegaard expert, Germagen, was right in his critique of the Soviet technocrats' dogmatic belief that they could plan everything, that they could calculate the consequences of their actions. He was also right when he spoke about being a victim of humanity's simpleminded belief in the triumphal progress of reason. I can feel how the foundation of my values has been kicked out from under me. Despite my rationalistic and sober-minded ideals, deep in my soul I have been a great romantic, a fool.

12

IT IS A CLICHÉ to claim that the return home is much harder than the departure. But it is true. I had hoped to slide gently back into my life at home, but instead I experience a crisis that I find much more difficult to recover from than the cold, the hunger, and the privation in the Siberian wilderness. During my long absence, I thought that the world I left would stay the same, that time and change only happened to me. But naturally, that is not how it is. Life takes it course everywhere, at home too.

This fact makes itself felt in the worst way: my girlfriend, Helene, has left me for another man, whom she says she loves and is now going to marry. He was there for her while I was out to save the Siberian hunters. My fur project was idealistic, she does not deny it, but when care and intimacy are an everyday need, idealism means almost nothing. It is certainly not the first time in my life that tragedy has struck, but this time I feel that my nerve center has been cauterized. Not only am I exhausted and lonely, but I go around with an agonizing sense of having neglected something vital: love. Helene became the heartbreak of my youth.

. . .

I contact Uffe, who has been struggling with his own problems. The Arab investor was not going away and had deluged him with phone calls day and night for several weeks. But when Shadrin's six thousand dollars finally arrived, Uffe had succeeded in calming the

The Siberian taiga.

Arab down and in setting up an installment agreement for the rest of the sum.

I go to Cambridge, isolate myself in one of the monk's cells at the university, and set about writing my PhD thesis on the Yukaghirs' spiritual beliefs. It takes me two years. In the meantime, I am profoundly lonely and disconsolate. At times, I cannot get out of bed and have to take all kinds of medications to keep myself going. At other times I get inspired and intoxicated with almost superhuman energy and write nonstop for weeks on end.

In my thesis, which is completed in 2003, and my subsequent book, *Soul Hunters,* published in 2007, the fur project is mentioned briefly in the foreword but is otherwise completely omitted.[1] This is probably because I cannot bear to think of all the disappointment that followed in its wake. Instead I describe the Siberia that I came to love: life as a hunter, the relationship to the spirits, and the just distribution of meat among the Yukaghirs. A romantic representation of my experiences? Perhaps. But holding on to the happy moments during my long stay in the taiga has probably been a question of mentally surviving the disappointment and the failures that cost me my love.

The Struggle against Bureaucracy

While I am writing, Uffe resumes collaboration with Shadrin on his own initiative. After the regime change in 2001, when the Sakha nationalist government was replaced by a more Moscow-oriented leadership, federal legislation gained more influence in Yakutia. So Shadrin thinks that now is the time to act, when it is easier to talk directly to the federal authorities, bypassing the Yakutian government.

In August 2003, Uffe travels to Yakutsk and spends three weeks in the offices of ministries and other state and regional authorities to find out what is possible and how to carry it out. Shadrin holds long discussions with the other members of the Council of Elders, which is the Yukaghirs' overall authority in Yakutsk, and finally presents an action plan and a budget, which later constitutes the core of an application for economic support for, among other things, hiring legal expertise.

As the fur project fundamentally deals with territorial and economic rights for aboriginal peoples, the application is sent to the organization IWGIA (International Work Group for Indigenous Affairs). Headquartered in Copenhagen, IWGIA's focus is on legal aid to reinforce the indigenous peoples' cultural and political struggle against the Yakutian bureaucracy for recognition and equality. At first, it goes really well, and in the half-year report Shadrin sounds optimistic.

In summer 2004, the reports become more seldom and less optimistic and finally cease. Shadrin has run into difficulties; the whole time he is met with the same unwillingness to cooperate and demands for more information. Obviously, there are forces of resistance somewhere in the system trying to tire him out by setting up new obstacles.

In September, Uffe travels to Yakutsk to monitor the project. Shadrin makes it plain that it is hopeless to stand alone against Sakhabult, and they discuss whether it would be an advantage for the fur project to involve the other indigenous minorities in Yakutia. At a meeting in the Russian Association of Indigenous Peoples of the North, RAIPON, Uffe proposes the establishment of a fund that will be commercially active and manage the collection and sale of the hunters' sable furs and distribute the profits among them. The proposal is well received and becomes the beginning of the Buyun corporation—the indigenous hunters' own trade association.

I myself do not return to Yakutsk until late summer in 2007. I have decided to write this memoir and am trying to find out what has happened to the hunters since I left the region seven years earlier. Both the distance of time and Uffe's positive reports about the development of the fur project have given me a renewed desire to come face-to-face with the world of Yakutian fur again.

In Sakhabult's Headquarters

With a certain unease, I land at the Yakutsk airport: I wonder whether I will be detained and sent on the next plane back to Moscow? Nikolayev has been replaced with a new president of the Sakha Republic —Vyacheslav Shtyrov, whose name the locals wryly pronounce so that it sounds like *strákhom,* which means "death penalty" in Russian —but I may have fallen into disfavor after the publication of my critical articles in *Ilken.* But my concern is completely unfounded. I get through passport control and walk into the arrivals hall, where voices and clattering luggage trolleys fill the air, mixed with the pedestrians' impatient steps.

An old acquaintance, Ruslan Skrybykin, steps out of the crowd and welcomes me heartily. In the last days of the crumbling Soviet Union, he worked as an English teacher in Nelemnoye, but now, like many other Russian intellectuals, he has gone private and has established his own translation firm in Yakutsk. Together we take a taxi to Sakhabult's headquarters in the hope of being granted an interview. Petrov is still the director of the firm. I wonder whether he will speak to me.

Again it turns out that I have been worrying unnecessarily. Petrov is in Moscow, and I am referred to the vice president of the firm, Nikolay Smetanin, who took over the post when Maksimov drowned. He is apparently unaware of my earlier conflict with Sakhabult, and I see no reason to make him aware of the old enmity. Smetanin is a large man who, despite his dark polyester suit, has powerful, broad hands, probably from many years of hard work. And indeed I find out that he is a former hunter. In the beginning he barely pays attention, only scarcely answering my questions, but when I tell him that I used to hunt the Kolyma region, he opens up with a warmth that only arises among colleagues.

It turns out that Sakhabult came under pressure after President Putin introduced a new antimonopoly law in 2006. The Yakutian state is no longer permitted to support Sakhabult, which must be open to competition from private firms. The result is that Sakhabult has officially been converted into a corporation. However, the Yakutian state currently owns all of the shares, so in reality the business is still a state enterprise. But several competing fur firms have sprung up as a result of the law, among them Maksimov's old company, Bulchut, and the aforementioned newly established firm, Buyun, which is managed by RAIPON. This has put pressure on fur prices, which have risen considerably. Today a hunter gets the equivalent of one hundred dollars for a sable fur.

Answering my question about why Sakhabult underpaid the hunters for so many years, Smetanin explains that Nikolayev forced the company to take over two bankrupt state enterprises, a fox farm and a shoe and leather factory, back in the 1990s. The president would not close them because they were heavily staffed and thereby ensured work for the locals. Sakhabult was given orders to keep running them under the circumstances of the new market economy, though without being permitted to lay off the many unneeded employees. These enterprises required immensely expensive investments in new technology, leather processing and tanning machines from Italy, and it was the indigenous trappers who paid for the business venture in the form of absurdly low fur prices.

Unfortunately, both the fox farm and the shoe and leather factory are still loss-making enterprises, and Smetanin himself expresses doubt as to whether it was reasonable to exploit the hunters so ruthlessly to keep the two productions going when they are quite clearly incapable of surviving. But, as he expresses it, "We didn't have any choice. The president had given his orders."

Mafia Methods or Not

It is always healthy to be presented with several perspectives on the same issue, and when I leave Sakhabult's headquarters, it is with a somewhat different impression of the company than the evil one I have carried around over the years. Sakhabult may be a Mafia-like enterprise that has no qualms about using brutality and violence to enforce its own interests, but that is how it is with almost all Russian businesses operating in the cowboy economy after the collapse of the Soviet Union. As a state enterprise, Sakhabult had obviously been under pressure from several sides and forced to follow difficult and tortuous paths to survive the forces of the free market.

The next day, I go to RAIPON's headquarters, where the people behind Buyun have their operation. The building is made of concrete in the shape of an enormous tepee painted with stylistic zigzag patterns in all the colors of the rainbow. The building alone gives an impression of a world closed around itself, long since disconnected from the lives of the hunters in the taiga. I am referred to a secretary, who, with a forced smile, asks me to take my place among the row of people who wish to speak to Nikolay Nazarov, the director of Buyun.

After a good hour's wait, my turn has come. I step into the office and meet a young, well-groomed man in a white shirt, sitting behind an enormous flat-screen monitor. His appearance is not exactly friendly. On the contrary, I sense an underlying hardness and arrogance. On the wall is a framed diploma with the Russian flag and the logo of a large, patriotic bear—visible proof that Nazarov is a member of United Russia, a political movement that has sworn allegiance to President Putin.

Over the past couple of years, countless Russian celebrities, sports stars, and pop singers have joined United Russia, which to an alarming degree resembles the Communist Party of a previous era: membership of United Russia is now almost a prerequisite for promotion in any public office.

Without so much as raising his gaze from the computer and in a mildly irritated tone, Nazarov says, "What do you want? Speak up. I haven't got all day."

In the fewest of words, I explain who I am and my former involvement in the indigenous people's fur trade. Nazarov finally looks up over the computer screen and stares at me with a technocrat's professional coldness.

"So you're one of the people behind the Danish–Yukaghir Fur Project," Nazarov declares. "I have heard of you. I suppose you could say that our company, Buyun, is the natural continuation of your failed enterprise. Our objective is also to look after the hunters' best interests. Your project showed quite clearly that a single *obshchina,* such as the Yukaghir one, cannot stand alone. Only by having a large, joint organization can we stand up to Sakhabult. That's the objective of Buyun.

"In 2006 we succeeded in gathering a good five thousand furs, but hopefully it will be more this year. The problem is that Sakhabult is raising fur prices the whole time in an attempt to knock us out of the race. We are now trying to counteract that by entering into fifty-year contracts with the hunters. Then they can't suddenly just change sides and go back to Sakhabult."

"But it can hardly be in the hunters' interests to enter into such long contracts," I say, mildly indignant. "Presumably that means that not only the hunter himself but perhaps also his sons will be bound to the contract?"

"Exactly," replies Nazarov. "Few hunters act sensibly. They sell their furs to the highest bidder without consideration that they are supporting the wrong cause—that they are supporting an old Communist enterprise such as Sakhabult."

"What but the highest possible price should be in the hunters' interest?" I ask.

"To support the construction of the new Russia—Putin's Russia!" Nazarov points triumphantly to his diploma from United Russia. "There you see Russia's way forward. Soon the jackals and swindlers will be cleaned out. It is possible that in the short term the hunters will not receive the optimal price for their furs, but under us they will work to make Russia strong again!"

"But our idea with the fur project was precisely to give the Yukaghir hunters the optimal price for their furs so that along the way they could lay the economic foundation for increased independence. It doesn't seem as if that's what you're aiming for," I protest.

"No," replies Nazarov. "As our leader, Putin, once expressed it, Russia will never go and become like the United States and the United Kingdom, where liberal ideas have deep historical roots. Russia needs strong central leadership. This is the only way we can maintain order and drive the country forward."

The Angel of Fear

Lord save us! I become quite ill from listening to Nazarov speak. Is this really the fur project that I worked so hard for? Not on my life! It is run by the control freak Nazarov, who worships Putin with the same zeal the followers of Stalin showed. Both kinds of worship lead to political centralization, democratic backlash, and the repeal of any form of regional autonomy. This is as far as one can get from the democratic, cooperative enterprise we had in mind when we started our fur project.

I almost prefer Sakhabult's robber mentality to this technocratic, authoritarian regime that Nazarov is so eagerly promoting. I already sense a new angel of tyranny floating through the air. It is the angel of fear, which Russia knows all too well, where citizens live in constant dread of the system, which is only waiting to lay its clammy hand on their shoulders and say, "What have we here, my friend?" The horrors of the past repeat themselves, and this must be said again and again in the hope that somebody will listen and change course. But Nazarov does not listen. I can only pray that his black angel does not succeed in driving the starved and harassed hunters over the edge.

■ ■ ■

The meeting with Nazarov makes me at once depressed and sentimental. I walk through the park. Fall has arrived and has already begun to send everything into hibernation. Mosquitoes and stable flies have taken the first blow. In the air around me their last buzzing can be heard before they finally go belly up. And the plants have also gotten their first whiff of the cold. The dried wheat stalks that extend right out to the bank of the River Lena jut out withered and dark gray in color. Winter is at the door, and I am again reminded of the transience of everything.

I button my coat up to my throat and sit on a bench. Time passes, and my back gets a little cold, but I stay sitting there anyway. Soon I can feel my eyelids drooping. And I let them close. In my mind's eye I see Ivan's attentive gaze and Akulina's covered, and yet so open, face. And I see Shalugin with his little pouting mouth and the troll-like Igor Khan. There is no sadness in a single one of their faces. No agonizing looks, no sense of secret torment in any of their cheerful minds. I ask myself why I should feel regret if they do not. Perhaps they will manage through the cold after all. They have always done so.

Early in the morning I am woken by a peculiar dream. I see myself lying on a reindeer skin, dreaming that I am lying on a reindeer skin, dreaming that I am lying on a reindeer skin, dreaming. I sit up in my sleeping bag and know right away that I am still not awake. Then I jump from one dreamed reality to the next and to the next again in the space of a few seconds, but none of them offers anything but the same repetition.

When I finally come to myself and look around, I am lying on a reindeer skin in a large hide-covered tent, surrounded by a couple of Danish journalists and some local Chukchi. The wind whistles through numerous holes in the hide cover, which is stretched out over a large, dome-shaped skeleton of wooden poles. The cold, gloomy draft of air breathes through the whole of the oval space. I can no longer sleep, not so much because of the wind and my tent mates' snoring, but more because of my troublesome dream about being trapped in an endless series of reflections.

I put my clothes on and fumble my way through the dark tent and out onto the treeless tundra. Here I attempt to light a cigarette, but the wind is too strong. Instead I sit on one of the many jettisoned sleds and gaze at the grass-covered expanses, the stony ground, and the meandering line of the river out in the boundless nothingness.

It is fall of 2008, and I am on the Chukchi Peninsula. Over the past couple months, a crew of Danish journalists has been following the world famous Danish polar explorer Knud Rasmussen's old sled route around the whole of the Arctic world.[1] However, they themselves have traveled not by dogsled but by plane and helicopter. I joined the expedition in Chukotka, which is the northeastern outpost of Siberia, where Rasmussen was stopped in 1924 and sent back after crossing the whole of the Inuits' territory from Greenland to the Pacific Ocean.

For thousands of years, before any Europeans had turned up, Inuits and Chukchi traveled by dogsled across the ice-covered sea—or paddled in kayaks in ice-free periods—to exchange merchandise with each other.[2] Their ancient trade was blocked as a result of the conflict between the Communist East and the capitalist West during the Cold War. These circumstances also severed the Inuits' ties of kinship, which formerly stretched across the Bering Strait. Only now can Inuits again visit their tribespeople on the opposite shore.[3]

The most striking difference between the indigenous peoples on either side of the Bering Strait is that the Alaskan populations have abandoned their traditional way of life and language during the seventy years' separation. At least this is what the journalists tell me. They can hardly believe their eyes when, after a long drive with a tracked vehicle across the icy desert, they arrive at a Chukchi camp where people still live in hide-covered tents, dress in fur garments, and speak Chukchi.

As for myself, I am less impressed. I have traveled through so many wildernesses on countless tracked vehicles and even more sleds and I have seen so many indigenous hunters and reindeer herders who live in the same way that I find none of it unusual anymore. Is it because, after the many years in Siberia, I have finally become so familiar with the indigenous people and their way of life that I can no longer get excited about—and perhaps do not even notice—what makes them seem different and exotic? After all, people are only strange in the eyes of strangers. For those who live with the indigenous people year in and year out, they become friends and acquaintances, or even family, and in time their lives and beliefs become just as natural as the changing seasons.

■　■　■

Maybe this is how it is for me. Long after my return home to Denmark, Siberia still lives in me. Every time I am at the family's vacation house in Sweden, I go out to a special place in the forest and sacrifice cigarettes and vodka to the bear I shot. On Grandma Akulina's advice, I have placed its skull in a tree that faces west, the direction of the Land of Shadows. The bear has become my invisible friend and helper in the area, where I now wander about, hunting and fishing.

I also have my own little lake in the woods, which I regularly visit on my way to work at the Moesgaard Museum. I speak softly to the lake, ask it for help to get through the many challenges of daily life, and thank it by throwing a coin out into the blue-black water. To the outsider it may seem strange or even crazy, but for me it is both natural and necessary, if fortune is to aid me.

In my dreams, I have also seen Ivan's shrunken and broken body again. He lies there on the bunk with big, bulging eyes, with arms that are as thin and gnarled as twigs, and a chest so prominent that all his ribs are visible. He screams the whole time in extreme torment: "We're going to die, can't you see, we're going to die!" I wake up with the horror jangling in all my nerves and have to keep myself awake for hours before I dare go back to sleep.

In this way, Siberia is still recurrent, something that gives me solace and fills me with dread. Despite the fact that I grew up with sober-minded ideals based on reason, in my inmost soul I have become another person, and yet not one with the indigenous people of Siberia. They are hunters and reindeer herders who live a simple life but who at the same time always long for change and surprise; they are people who like to roam around in search of new hunting grounds, new opportunities, and adventures. For me, they fulfilled a youthful ideal, an attempt to cultivate the masculine identity of an adventurer who in his tireless hunt for new experiences endures one trial after the other, with death as his companion. The immense break from the familiar back home and the confrontation with the new and untested out there were once what made my life worth living.

But now I am in my late thirties and have both a wife and child. I no longer feel the desire to charge off to the ends of the earth. My mind is tired of the hard country, tired of the restlessness and the vagrant life and the many hazards it involves. I now have an insidious feeling of loneliness, a sense that something more essential, something vital, is being neglected back home. In this moment, out in the middle of the Siberian tundra, it becomes clear to me that I must go back—home to Astrid and little Akulina.

APPENDIXES: SURVIVING IN SIBERIA

Using the Leghold Trap

The leghold trap is what is known as a restraining trap. The metal jaws of the trap close around the animal's foreleg and hold it without killing it. The leghold trap exists in different, industrially manufactured sizes, number 0, 1, 2, and so on. The number indicates the size and striking power: the higher the number, the bigger the animal the trap can hold. There exist traps so powerful that they can hold a bear, but they are practically never used. It is most common to use leghold traps to catch animals of the weasel family—sables, mink, and wolverines—as well as animals such as wolves and foxes. However, the animal is sometimes alive when the hunter inspects the trap. If it is a sable or other small fur animal, the hunter kills it with a tight squeeze to the chest. Large animals such as wolverines and wolves are shot through the head. The idea is to damage the pelt as little as possible.

1. The hunter shovels a pile of snow beside the sable track. He pats the pile of snow together well with the ski before he digs into it.
2. The hunter cuts a vertical slit with his ski in one side of the pile of snow and digs a hollow in it.

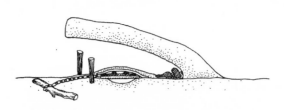

3. At the inner end of the hollow, the hunter places the bait: a chunk of moose meat or a piece of fish. In front of the bait he digs a little depression, lays some sticks lengthwise, and places the set trap on top. This prevents the trap getting frozen into the snow so that it does not work. For the same reason, he lays a thin sheet of paper over the trap, and lastly he covers the whole thing with loose snow. The trap itself is affixed with a branch through the chain of the trap. As a last trick, the hunter places a small stick on each side of the trap so that the sable is forced to climb over it when it tries to reach the bait.

4. The trap can be made extra attractive for the sable by sprinkling small pieces of bait on the roof.

Yukaghir Idols

Here are three different wooden Yukaghir idols, each about 1.2 inches wide and 6.3 to 7.5 inches in height. All three idols carry a Christian crucifix to fight off evil spirits, and all must be fed regularly with bone marrow from killed prey.

The one on the left is "Owner of the House" (Yukaghir, *nu'mon-pogil'*) or "Father Fire" (Yukaghir, *lo'cin-coro'mo*), who protects the home or the encampment from evil spirits. He is often described as a naked baby, which is why he has no hair on his head. He is said to warn the household by making crackling noises, like the crackling of burning wood.

The one on the right is the head of the evil spirits, the "Grand-

father with the Pointed Head" (Yukaghir, *yiodeiis'ien'ulben*). This figure is placed next to a sleeping infant; if an evil spirit approaches the child, the spirit will recognize the child as one of its own kind and leave it alone.

The idol in the middle is a representation of the hunter's soul, *ayibii*. It is depicted as half man, half moose, since it must take the bodily appearance of a moose when it travels to the house of its spiritual owner during the hunter's dream, in much the same way as the hunter does when attempting to seduce a moose in waking life.

Netting Fish in Siberia

A rope is tied to the end of a tree trunk, which is floated under the ice through a row of holes in a straight line; then a fishing net is tied to one end of the rope and pulled in under the ice by the other end.

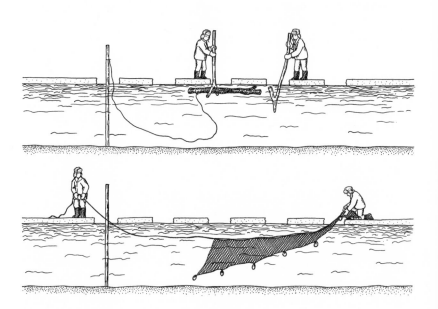

Finding Your Way in the Taiga

Maps of the wilderness areas of northeastern Siberia are very rough and difficult to use to find your way. And, on the whole, they are difficult to procure. So the hunters do not use maps but learn to know each hunting area by walking back and forth through it until they are familiar with all of its distinguishing features. These may consist of special trees, a certain hill formation, a lake—whatever is distinctive.

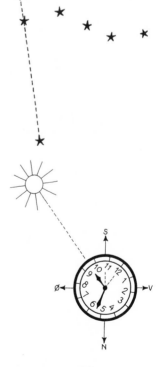

Nor do the hunters use compasses. This is because the taiga is so dense and inaccessible that it is difficult to keep to a compass course. You have to weave through the forest. If the hunter needs to find a direction, he can make use of nature in the following various ways.

On a clear night, the North Star is always a loyal aid. It is big and bright and always points—as the name says—to the north. All of the stars in the sky revolve around the North Star. It is easy to find your way with the help of the Great Bear constellation. If you draw an imaginary line between two of the stars, it passes through a large, glittering star higher up: this is the North Star.

On a clear day, if you have a watch that is keeping reasonably good time, you can use the sun. When it is twelve o'clock, the sun is always in the south. At other times, you turn the watch so that the little hand points toward the sun and then find the point midway between this and twelve: this point is south. The method is not quite as accurate as a compass, but it can be used. Vegetation can also provide an indication of direction. In mountain forest, as a rule, the trees have stronger branches on the southerly side. The same applies to hillocks on the landscape, where the plants grow more strongly on the south-facing side.

How to Track and Shoot a Moose

Which Direction Has the Moose Gone?

If snow cover is thin, there are often clear imprints of the hooves in the track, and the direction the moose is traveling is obvious. When conditions are favorable, you can also form an impression of how fast the moose has been moving. Moose spread their hooves when walking fast and when running. The faster the gait, the greater the spread.

 · If the snow is loose, the imprints are as a rule unclear, and you have to try to determine the direction in another way. Snow will always be more compressed in the foremost part of the hooves and thus indicates the direction of movement of the animal.

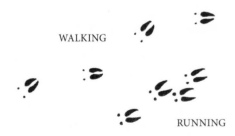

WALKING

RUNNING

Reading moose tracks: patterns of moose tracks reveal how fast and in what direction the animal was moving.

How Old Is the Track?

If the edge of snow around a track is sharp, it is often less than twenty-four hours old. If the edge if rounded, it is older and not worth following.

Cow or Bull?

Bull moose as a rule are larger than cows and so leave relatively larger hoofprints. But it can be difficult to determine the size of the moose from the hoofprint alone, and prints in snow often seem bigger than they really are.

If you find urine along the track, it is easier to determine the sex of the animal. Traces of urine close to the forelegs indicate a bull; if the urine imprint is closer to the hind legs, it is a cow.

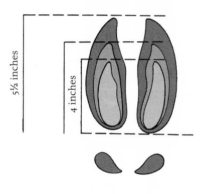

Full-grown bull: track longer than 5½ inches.
Young bull or full-grown cow: track measures 4 to 5½ inches.
Calf: track shorter than 4 inches.

Shooting a Moose

The moose must be hit in the region of the heart and lungs for the shot to be fatal. This picture series shows how the position of the moose can significantly influence the accuracy of the hunter's fire.

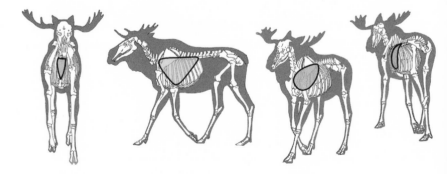

Preface and Acknowledgments

1. *The Last of the Yukaghirs* (Nordisk Film, 1998).
2. Waldemar Jochelson, *The Yukaghir and the Yukaghirized Tungus*, Publications of the Jesup North Pacific Expedition, Memoirs of the American Museum of Natural History, vol. 9, ed. Franz Boas (New York: American Museum of Natural History, 1926).

One Last, Feeble Attempt

1. Andrew Jack, *Inside Putin's Russia* (London: Granta Books, 2004), 203.

1. Shalugin, Leader of the Yukaghirs

1. Hudson's Bay and Annings Limited, in association with V/O Sojuzpushnina, *The Fur Bearing Mammals of the Soviet Union* (London: Hudson's Bay and Annings Limited, in association with V/O Sojuzpushnina, 1983), 30.
2. Yuri Slezkine, "Savage Christians or Unorthodox Russians? The Missionary Dilemma in Siberia," in *Between Heaven and Hell: The Myth of Siberia in Russian Culture*, ed. Galya Diment and Yuri Slezkine (New York: St. Martin's Press, 1993), 15–31.
3. Svend Aage Christensen and Knud Rasmussen, *Rusland 1689: Verdenshistorie 21* [Russia 1689: World history 21] (Copenhagen: Forlaget Danmark, 1992), 202–6.
4. Waldemar Jochelson, *The Yakut*, Anthropological Papers of the American Museum of Natural History, vol. 33, part 2 (New York: American Museum of Natural History, 1933), 181–85.
5. Slezkine, "Savage Christians or Unorthodox Russians?" 17.
6. Andreas P. Hovgaard, *Nordenskiölds rejse omkring Asien og Europa* [Nordenskiöld's expedition around Asia and Europe] (Copenhagen: Forlagsbureauet i Kjøbenhavn, 1881), 134.

2. A Post-Soviet Nightmare

1. Ronald G. Suny, *The Revenge of the Past: Nationalism, Revolution and the Collapse of the Soviet Union* (Stanford, Calif.: Stanford University Press, 1993), 55.
2. Varlam Shalamov, *Kolyma Tales*, trans. John Glad (Harmondsworth: Penguin Books, 1994).
3. *Rusland: Samling eller sammenbrud?* [Russia: Unity or collapse?], ed. Jens-Jørgen Jensen and Märta-Lisa Magnusson (Esbjerg, Denmark: Sydjysk Universitetsforlag, 1995), 181.
4. George Kennan, *Tent Life in Siberia: Adventures among the Koraks and Other Tribes in Kamchatka and North Asia* (New York: Putnam and Sons, 1871), 116.

3. Sable Furs for Sale

1. Nikolay I. Spiridonov (Teki Odulok), "Odulu (Yukagiru) Kolumskogo Okruga" [The Odul (Yukaghirs) of the Kolyma region] (Yakutsk: Institute for the Problem of the Small Peoples of the North, 1996 [originally published in *Sovetskiy Sever* 9–12 (1930)]), 167–214.
2. Victor A. Shnirelman, "Introduction: North Eurasia," in *Encyclopaedia of Hunters and Gatherers*, ed. Richard B. Lee and Richard Daly (Cambridge: Cambridge University Press, 1999), 119.
3. Nikolay Vakhtin, *The Yukaghir Language in Sociolinguistic Perspective* (Leningrad: Institute for Linguistics, Academy of Science, 1991).
4. Janet Martin, *Treasure of the Land of Darkness: The Fur Trade and Its Significance for Medieval Russia* (Cambridge: Cambridge University Press, 1986).
5. Robert J. Kerner, *The Urge to the Sea: The Course of Russian History. The Role of Rivers, Portages, Ostrogs, Monasteries, and Furs* (New York: Russell and Russell 1942), 30.
6. Benson Bobrick, *East of the Sun: The Conquest and Settlement of Siberia* (London: Heinemann, 1992), 68.
7. Oleg V. Bychkov, "Russian Hunters in Eastern Siberia in the Seventeenth Century: Lifestyle and Economy," trans. Mina A. Jacobs, *Arctic Anthropology* 31, 1 (1994): 72–85.
8. Bobrick, *East of the Sun*, 72.
9. Raymond H. Fisher, *The Russian Fur Trade 1550–1700*, University of California Publications in History, vol. 31 (Berkeley: University of California Press, 1943), 207.
10. René Grousset, *The Empire of the Steppes: A History of Central Asia* (New Brunswick, N.J.: Rutgers University Press, 1970), 586 n 106.
11. Ibid., 117.
12. Fisher, *The Russian Fur Trade*, 209.

13. James Forsyth, *A History of the Peoples of Siberia: Russia's North Asian Colony 1581–1990* (Cambridge: Cambridge University Press, 1992), 247.
14. Eske Willerslev, "Sibiriens Naturmiljø" [The natural environment of Siberia], in *På Rejse i Sibirien: Tre danske ekspeditioners møde med Nordøstsibiriens jægere og nomader* [Exploring Siberia: Three Danish expeditions' encounter with the hunters and nomads of northeastern Siberia], ed. Rane Willerslev et al. (Højbjerg: Moesgaard Museum, 1995), 48.
15. Rane Willerslev, "Urbanites without City: Three Generations of Siberian Yukaghir Women," *Acta Borealia* 27, 2 (2010): 197.
16. *15 let, Sakhabult po puti reform* [15 years, Sakhabult on the road of reforms] (Yakutsk: Sakhabult, 2007).
17. Erik Sander, "Hunting/Trapping/Fishing," in *Sibérie II: Questions sibériennes* (Paris: Institute d'Études Slaves, 1993), 244.
18. Ibid.
19. Rane Willerslev and Olga Ulturgasheva, "The Sable Frontier: The Siberian Fur Trade as Montage," *Cambridge Anthropology* 26, 2 (2006/2007): 86.
20. Rane Willerslev, *Hunting and Trapping in Siberia* (Copenhagen: Arctic Information, 2000).
21. Sevyan Vainshtein, "The Turkic Peoples, Sixth to Twelfth Centuries," in *Nomads of Eurasia*, ed. Vladimir N. Basilov (Seattle and London: Natural History Museum of Los Angeles County in Association with University of Washington Press, 1989), 55–66.
22. Alexei P. Okladnikov, "Ancient Population of Siberia and Its Culture," in *The Peoples of Siberia*, ed. Maksim G. Levin and Leonid P. Potapov (Chicago: University of Chicago Press, 1956), 87–90.
23. Jochelson, *The Yakut*, 131.
24. Sergey A. Tokarev and I. S. Gurvich, "The Yakuts," in *The Peoples of Siberia*, ed. Levin and Potapov, 276–77.
25. Waldemar Jochelson, *Peoples of Asiatic Russia* (New York: American Museum of Natural History, 1928), 27.
26. Rane Willerslev, *Soul Hunters: Hunting, Animism, and Personhood among the Siberian Yukaghirs* (Berkeley: University of California Press, 2007), 37.
27. Wacław Sieroszewski, *Yakutu: Opyt etnograficheskogo issledovaniya* [The Yakuts: Experience of the Ethnographic Research], 2d ed. (1896; Moscow: Moskva, 1993), 356.

4. Out of Range

1. Tim Ingold, "Hunting, Sacrifice and the Domestication of Animals," in *The Appropriation of Nature: Essays on Human Ecology and Social Relations* (Manchester: University of Manchester, 1986), 258.

2. Rane Willerslev and Morten Axel Pedersen, "Proportional Holism: Joking the Cosmos into the Right Shape in North Asia," in *Experiments in Holism: Theory and Practice in Contemporary Anthropology*, ed. Ton Otto and Nils Bubandt (Oxford: Wiley-Blackwell, 2010), 270.

5. *Soft Gold*

1. Trevor Day, *Taiga* (Austin, Tex.: Raintree, 2003), 10–11.
2. Rane Willerslev, "Spirits as 'Ready to Hand': A Phenomenological Analysis of Yukaghir Knowledge and Dreaming," *Anthropological Theory* 4, 4 (2004): 195–418.
3. M. V. Stepanova, I. S. Gurvich, and V. V. Khramova, "The Yukagirs," in *The Peoples of Siberia*, trans. Stephen P. Dunn and Ethel Dunn, ed. M. G. Levin and L. P. Potapov (Chicago: Chicago University Press, 1964), 796.

6. *Starvation and Desperation*

1. Willerslev, *Hunting and Trapping in Siberia*.
2. Jochelson, *The Yukaghir and the Yukaghirized Tungus*, 45.
3. Willerslev, *Soul Hunters*, 110–11.

7. *In the Yukaghirs' Camp*

1. Sherwood L. Washburn and Chet S. Lancaster, "The Evolution of Hunting," in *Man the Hunter*, ed. R. B. Lee and I. DeVore (New York: Aldine De Gruyter, 1968), 293.
2. Raymond A. Dart, "The Predatory Transition from Ape to Man," *International and Linguistic Review* 1 (1953): 201–17. See also Matt Cartmill, *A View to a Death in the Morning: Hunting and Nature through History* (Cambridge, Mass., and London: Harvard University Press, 1993), 1–27.
3. John G. Mitchell, "Our Wily White-Tailed Deer: Elegant but Perplexing Neighbors," *Smithsonian*, November 1982, 140.
4. Cartmill, *A View to a Death in the Morning*, 69.
5. Eduardo Viveiros de Castro, "Cosmological Deixis and Amerindian Perspectivism," *Journal of the Royal Anthropological Institute* (N.S.) 4 (1998): 469–88.
6. Waldemar Bogoras, *The Chukchee*, publications of the Jesup North Pacific Expedition, Memoirs of the American Museum of Natural History, vol. 7, ed. Franz Boas (New York: American Museum of Natural History, 1904–9), 281.
7. Valérie Chaussonnet, "Needles and Animals: Women's Magic," in *Crossroads of Continents: Cultures of Siberia and Alaska*, ed. William W. Fitzhugh and Aron Crowell (Washington, D.C.: Smithsonian Institution, 1988), 209–27.

8. Willerslev, *Soul Hunters,* 89–90.
9. Ibid., 70–79.
10. Barbara Noske, *Beyond Boundaries: Humans and Animals* (Montreal: Black Rose Books, 1997).
11. Claude Lévi-Strauss, *The Raw and the Cooked,* Mythologiques, vol. 1 (Chicago: University of Chicago Press, 1983).
12. Tim Ingold, "Humanity and Animality," in *Companion Encyclopedia of Anthropology: Humanity, Culture and Social Life,* ed. Tim Ingold (London and New York: Routledge, 1994), 30.
13. Erica Fudge, *Animal* (London: Reaction Books, 2002), 128, 138.
14. Thomas Nagel, "What Is It Like to Be a Bat?" in *Mortal Questions* (Cambridge: Cambridge University Press, 1997), 165–80.
15. Barbara Bodenhorn, "Person, Place and Parentage: Ecology, Identity and Social Relations on the North Slope of Alaska," in *Arctic Ecology and Identity,* ed. S. A. Mousalimas (Budapest: Akadémia Kiadó, and Los Angeles: International Society for Trans-Oceanic Research, 1997), 171.
16. David M. Smith, "An Athapaskan Way of Knowing: Chipewyan Ontology," *American Ethnologist* 25, 3 (1998): 412–32. See also Jean-Guy A. Goulet, *Ways of Knowing: Experience, Knowledge and Power among the Dene Tha* (Lincoln: University of Nebraska Press, 1998).
17. Maurice Bloch, *How We Think They Think: Anthropological Approaches to Cognition, Memory, and Literacy* (Boulder, Colo.: Westview Press, 1998).

8. A Long-Awaited Friend

1. Yuri Slezkine, *Arctic Mirrors: Russia and the Small Peoples of the North,* (Ithaca and London: Cornell University Press, 1994), 27.
2. Bogoras, *The Chukchee,* 688.
3. Ibid., 693–97.
4. Ibid.
5. Ibid.
6. Jochelson, *The Yukaghir and the Yukaghirized Tungus,* 57.
7. Stepanova, Gurvich, and Khramova, "The Yukagirs," 788–98.

9. The Curse

1. Piers Vitebsky, *Reindeer People: Living with Animals and Spirits in Siberia* (London: HarperCollins Publishers, 2005), 277–80.
2. Jochelson, *The Yukaghir and the Yukaghirized Tungus,* 58.
3. Alexander Pika, "The Spatial-Temporal Dynamic of Violent Death among the Native Peoples of Northern Russia," trans. Eugenia W. Davis, ed. Igor I. Krupnik, *Arctic Anthropology* 30, 2 (1993): 61–67.

4. Jochelson, *The Yukaghir and the Yukaghirized Tungus,* 146.
5. Ibid., 165–67.
6. Spiridonov, "Odulu (Yukagiru) Kolumskogo Okruga," 50–52.
7. Stanley A. Freed, Ruth S. Freed, and Laila Williamson, "The American Museum's Jesup North Pacific Expedition," in *Crossroads of Continents: Cultures of Siberia and Alaska,* ed. William W. Fitzhugh and Aron Crowell (Washington, D.C.: Smithsonian Institution 1988), 97–104.
8. Ibid., 51.
9. Thomas Ross Miller, "Object Lessons: Wooden Spirits, Wax Voices, and Collecting the Folk," in *Properties of Culture – Culture as Property: Pathways to Reform in Post-Soviet Siberia,* ed. Erich Kasten (Berlin: Dietrich Reimer Verlag, 2004), 196.

10. Land of Shadows

1. Stepanova, Gurvich, and Khramova, "The Yukagirs," 788–98.
2. Slezkine, *Arctic Mirrors,* 233.
3. Caroline Humphrey with Urgunge Onon, *Shamans and Elders: Experience, Knowledge, and Power among Dauer Mongols* (Oxford: Clarendon Press, 1996), 48–49.
4. Mircea Eliade, *Shamanism: Archaic Techniques of Ecstasy* (Princeton, N.J.: Princeton University Press, 1964).
5. A. F. Anisimov, "The Shaman's Tent of the Evenks and the Origin of the Shamanic Rite," in *Studies in Siberian Shamanism,* ed. Henry N. Michael (Toronto: University of Toronto Press, 1963), 84–123; I. S. Vodovin, "Social Foundations of Ancestor Cult among the Yukaghirs, Koryaks and the Chukchis," in *Shamanism in Siberia,* ed. Vilmos Dioszegi and Mihaly Hoppal (Budapest: Adamediai Kiado, 1978), 405–18.
6. Nikolai Ssorin-Chaikov, "Evenki Shamanic Practices in Soviet Present and Ethnographic Present Perfect," *Anthropology of Consciousness* 12, 1 (2001): 1–18.
7. Willerslev, *Soul Hunters,* 136–40.
8. Jochelson, *The Yukaghir and the Yukaghirized Tungus.*
9. Z. V. Gogolev et al., *Yukagiru: Istoriko-etnograficheskiy ocherk* [The Yukaghirs: an ethnohistorical outline] (Novosibirsk: Nauka, 1975); V. A. Tugolukov, *Kto vy Yukagiriy?* [Who are you Yukaghirs?] (Moscow: Nauka, 1979).
10. Willerslev, *Soul Hunters,* 50.
11. Gananath Obeyesekere, "Foreword: Reincarnation Eschatologies and the Comparative Study of Religions," in *Amerindian Rebirth: Reincarnation Belief among North American Indians and Inuit,* ed. Antonia Mills and Richard Slobodin (Toronto: University of Toronto Press, 1994), xi–xxiv.

12. Lee Guemple, "The Inuit Cycle of Spirits," in *Amerindian Rebirth,* ed. Mills and Slobodin, 107–22.

13. Jim Tucker, *Life before Life: A Scientific Investigation of Children's Memories of Previous Lives* (New York: St. Martin's Press, 2005).

11. Screwed

1. Rane Willerslev, "Datsko-Yukagirskiy pushnoy proyekt" [The Danish–Yukaghir fur project], *Ilken* 7, 10 (2000): 5.

2. Igor Kolomets [Rane Willerslev], "Kogda vy nam zaplotite za nashu pushninu, Sakhabult?" [When will you pay us for our fur, Sakhabult?], *Ilken* 8, 11 (2000): 8.

12. The Way Back

1. Rane Willerslev, "In-Between Self and Other: Hunting, Perception and Personhood among the Upper Kolyma Yukaghirs of North-Eastern Siberia" (PhD diss., University of Cambridge, 2004); Willerslev, *Soul Hunters.*

A Leap in Time

1. Knud Rasmussen, "Intellectual Culture of the Iglulik Eskimos," in *Report of the Fifth Thule Expedition 1921–24,* vol. 7 (Copenhagen: Gyldendalske Boghandel, Nordisk Forlag, 1929).

2. William W. Fitzhugh and Aron Crowell, *Crossroads of Continents: Cultures of Siberia and Alaska* (Washington, D.C.: Smithsonian Institution Press, 1988).

3. Adele Barker, "The Divided Self: Yuri Rytkheu and Contemporary Chukchi Literature," in *Between Heaven and Hell: Myth of Siberia in Russian Culture,* ed. Galya Diment and Yuri Slezkine (New York: St. Martin's Press, 1993), 215–26.

RANE WILLERSLEV is professor of anthropology and director of the Museum of Cultural History at the University of Oslo. His primary field of research is hunting and spiritual knowledge among Siberia's indigenous peoples. He is the author of *Soul Hunters: Hunting, Animism, and Personhood among the Siberian Yukaghirs.*

COILÍN ÓHAISEADHA is a freelance translator and professional storyteller with a long-standing interest in wilderness survival skills.